FINDING BALANCE
A Mother's Journey to Inner Peace

FINDING BALANCE

A Mother's Journey
to Inner Peace

~

KELLY SWIERSKI LOIODICE

Cover and Book Design: Ron Carter
Cover Development: Genevieve Cerasoli
Henna Art: Saima Ajmal, Warwick Henna

Please note that some names have been changed within this book to offer individuals anonymity. The loved ones in my life shared themselves without knowing that I would want to share my story beyond my roots. My journey is my own, as is my voice, and I only speak for myself from my own heart, not for the ashram or any other person noted.

For the Eternal Mother in each of us

To search elsewhere
for what you already
hold in your hand
is fruitless.

⁓Bhagawan Nityananda

When you come
to the realization
'That which I seek
is not outside,
but is within myself,'
there is an experience
of ananda, of joy, within.

⁓Mahamandaleshwar Swami Nityananda

INTRODUCTION

AS I STOOD on the rim of a sunken stretch of land in a tiny village in India, I began to contemplate. What really brought me here, half a world away from my husband and two young daughters? What drew me to a place where I didn't speak the language, where my feet were on unfamiliar ground? Why were my mind and heart finally at ease? I smiled as I started connecting the dots in my mind.

I glimpsed at the hard, dry dirt under my sneakers and took a step toward the center of the recess where natural hot springs arose. Inky slabs of stone surrounded scattered puddles of liquid and patchy spots of thick greenery. The dark earth lining the water looked as if it had been charred, like lava had once flowed from these fountains leaving behind a rich, black floor.

I leaned toward a strip of lanky, emerald grasses and clapped my hands to ward off any bloodthirsty reptiles, and a woman in a magenta silk top and tightly wrapped skirt stopped walking and peered at me from about twenty feet away. She was balancing a sealed, round basket on top of her head—the perfect spot for a giant, coiled king cobra. I grimaced and raised my hand apologetically, immediately regretting drawing attention to myself and disturbing the passage of venomous royalty. Then I turned my head away and breathed in the warm, dry air.

Only one more day left, I reminded myself. Although I knew my world would soon return to the familiar garter snake and mushy family hug, I also knew that I had begun a journey I would follow with each breath for the rest of my life. I needed to soak in every last moment as I realized my time in India would soon be just a memory.

I scanned the area before me and became captivated by the other women walking the charcoal earth. Their hair was nestled in buns or tucked under the wicker splinters of a basket. They were dressed in brilliant colored skirts and tops and wore sandals or went without shoes. I looked down at my wrinkled, white T-shirt and baggy, beige capris. The differences in our appearance were obvious, as were the differences in our languages, our customs, even our meals. White rice could never substitute for al-dente pasta back home.

Yet in such a foreign place, I felt like I belonged. Somehow, I fit, like an odd piece of a puzzle that looks as if it will never connect but actually joins perfectly and completes a beautiful picture. I knew that I was an intricate part of this unfamiliar land. The union I felt wasn't visible on the outside; it stemmed from some deep place within me. I began to wonder whether the lady with the cobra on her head had felt the connection too and if I'd missed a faint, perceptive smile in her gaze.

I shifted my attention from the beautiful women walking the arid opening in front of me to a majestic mountain in the distance. The leafy trees dotting its terrain made it seem lush, and its wide girth anchored it solidly into the earth. As I stared at the magnificent mass, I realized its sturdiness stemmed from a broad area of balance, and it reminded me of the posture *tadasana*, the mountain pose, from a recent yoga class. In the stance, I had stood firmly on both feet, rooting myself into the ground. I knew that I needed to retain that same firm foundation when I returned home to my family and all of the nooks and crannies in life. Somehow, I needed to remain full and balanced within beyond any physical form. Somehow, I needed to take India back with me.

Twenty years earlier, I explored a different kind of place in search of balance and fullness...

As I lifted my frosty mugs from the wet bar and weaved my way through a boisterous crowd, balance didn't stem from any feeling on the inside. It came from my gross ability to keep my hands and body steady and my mugs of beer full—challenging in a cramped, dark, smoke-filled room teeming with loud music and the faint smell of pizza.

"Jim, move to the left. I can't put these beers down until you lean over," I said, nudging my elbow into my dark-haired Italian boyfriend's back.

Jim glanced up at me and shifted his broad obtrusive shoulders to one side. Then I lifted the mugs over him as if I were carrying melted gold and gingerly placed them on the shiny table, already wet from previous beer runs.

"Great, not a drop spilled. I should be getting a nice tip from this table."

"Just add it to my tab," he replied, smiling and rolling his eyes.

"You know, you're going to have to settle up one of these days."

"Don't worry. I've got you covered. I'm just surprised you didn't bail on the drinks and hit the bar for a dance while you were up there."

I listened to the sounds of Fleetwood Mac booming from

the jukebox and eyed the old wooden bar with cat-like determination. Then I raised my arms in the air and wiggled my hips.

"Guess I needed the right song. Let's go back so you can give me a boost."

"Wouldn't have it any other way." Jim reached his arm around my waist and drew me close as my friends laughed and followed my lead, rocking in their seats.

The laughter and company of young, drunk friends intoxicated my spirit and seemed to offer all that I needed as a mere twenty-something. Balance seemed much easier to grasp in the handles of beer mugs and winding trips around a bar back then. When my cold brews were replaced by midnight feedings and juice boxes for my children, I felt my self-centered, carefree life end. I went from a self-absorbed happy-hour lover to a sleep-deprived, boo-boo-kissing mother bouncing to meet the changing needs of my family. I continued to remain steady on the outside, even as I carried car seats, book bags, groceries, and children in my arms, grateful for the practice I had carrying drinks. But deep down, I knew that my physical sense of equilibrium had relatively nothing to do with my internal sense, and I began to understand the profound meaning of the word balance and the need for more of it in my life.

With the vines of motherhood wrapped tightly around my heart, I started to search for wisdom beyond the conversation sparked over frosty mugs and pursue paths that offered a more lasting sense of contentment. My journey led me to India and beyond; ultimately, to places within me that I never knew existed.

My story begins years ago, in the heat of summer, on the sands of the Jersey Shore…

I

FIRST SPARKS, GURUS, AND ORANGE SODA

1

AS I SLIPPED my feet out of my red, rubbery flip-flops and into the silky sand, I felt the culmination of the morning's hot sun on my soles. The sand felt like a hot griddle beneath me, and I started to dance, as if the quick lifting of each foot would really make a difference.

My husband, Jim, was behind me lugging our bulky red-and-white cooler stocked with juicy peaches, salami sandwiches, and ice-cold beer. He was wearing his favorite blue and green swim trunks that were just starting to fade and fray above his knees, having seen countless wipeouts at the shore's edge. As I turned to face him, my eyes were drawn to his bare chest and strong arms. His work outdoors as an excavator had allowed the sun to tattoo a tan line on his upper arms outlining the edge of an invisible short-sleeve shirt. He smirked and shook his head as he watched me dance in the sand. Then he dropped the cooler to the ground and waited for direction.

I turned back toward the beach and scanned the area in front of us, pointing to an open spot between a small family and an elderly couple. Jim lifted the cooler and followed me, leaving his flip-flops on until he reached the place where I had dropped our

Mexican beach blanket. Moments later, I sank into my squatty chair, and the delicious fragrance of coconut suntan lotion enveloped me. Jim sat down next to me and squeezed my hand.

"Perfect start to our vacation," he said, adjusting his sunglasses. "I could get used to this way of life."

I smiled and nodded my head in agreement, feeling as if I could remain right in this spot, melting into my beach chair for the entirety of our vacation—or longer. "I don't know why we haven't given up our jobs, sold everything we owned, and already moved here," I said.

"Me neither. Maybe the million dollar price tag has something to do with it, but we can dream." Jim dug into the cooler and grabbed two cans of beer, pouring the amber liquid into shiny plastic cups. "Here you go," he said, handing a cup to me.

As I brought the cup to my lips, I let the suds form a frothy mustache. I tapped Jim's shoulder, and as he turned to face me, I smiled and licked the mustache away slowly.

"You're already making me want more than just a beer," he intimated in a low voice, leaning in to kiss me.

As our lips parted, my desire for him lingered. I leaned back in my chair and closed my eyes. The sound of the crashing surf filled the air around me, and I began to comb the smooth sand with my fingertips. My mind eased into stillness until the deep clanging sound of a bell drew my attention back toward the beach entrance. A tanned man in white shorts and sandals stood at the edge of the wooden walkway, ringing a bell like a church calling to its hungry devotees, beckoning beachgoers to the ice cream truck he had parked nearby. I looked over at Jim, who was already reaching into one of our beach bags for money.

"Want anything?" he asked.

"I think I feel like a cherry Italian ice."

"Okay. I'll see if they have that. If not, I'll surprise you."

I winked at him, appreciating how well he knew me. We had

been married for over five years and had dated through high school and college. As my mind wandered to the moment I first introduced myself to him, it seemed like yesterday…

Standing in my high school hallway and leaning against a row of cold, metal lockers, I watched a handsome, mustached Italian boy spin a combination a couple of feet away. I ran my fingers through my feathered-back brown hair and adjusted the stylish black mesh overlay that covered my fluorescent-pink shirt. (It was the '80s and Madonna had revolutionized my sense of fashion.) As I pretended to look away, I hoped he hadn't seen me eyeing him.

Jim opened his locker and crouched down to get something off the bottom. He seemed so vulnerable there—like an unaware bird in a nest, clueless about the bold, brazen owl ready to swoop in and grab him. As he reached for a book, I followed my instinct, stepped toward him, and pushed him over. He looked up at me completely stunned and then burst out in laughter. We met again at a friend's party a few weeks later and shared our first kiss.

From then on, I waited for Jim's call every night, ultimately tying up my family's single phone line for hours while I talked with my new boyfriend. We wrote notes to each other in class and passed the scraggly fringed papers in school hallways. We doodled hearts with our names on them in notebooks. Jim was more polite and romantic than any of the other guys I had dated. He sent roses to me at school, even though we went there together, and he opened my car door for me before I hopped into his shiny black Chevy pickup truck every Friday and Saturday night. I was head over heels for this strong, yet most gentle, upper classman. Even then, I had a deep knowing that Jim was the one for me.

"Hey, where are you? Back to planet earth," Jim said, walking toward me with our frozen treats in hand.

"Jesus, my brain was off in the hallways of our high school," I laughed. "It doesn't seem that long ago, even though there's probably a reunion lurking somewhere around the corner. Do you remember the day we first met?"

"You mean when you pushed my ass to the floor? Yeah, of course I remember that. I've been enjoying your ass-pushing every day since then." He bent down and kissed me again.

I opened my cherry flavored ice and used the wooden stick to scoop the melting slush from the sides first. It tasted so tangy and sweet that I could almost feel it staining my lips a rich shade of scarlet. I reached into my striped beach bag, grabbed a magazine, and began skimming the cover. Before I turned a page, my eyes were drawn to the treasure hunters fingering through the sand at the ocean's edge. I let my imagination run wild as I pictured old coins from sunken ships washing ashore and watched for signs reminiscent of Charlie uncovering the golden ticket to the Chocolate Factory. Jim interrupted my day dreaming after he finished his ice cream.

"Are you ready to hit the water?"

I glimpsed tiny streams of sweat running down the sides of his face and readily grabbed his hand. "Let's go. I'd race you, but I think you'd melt into the sand before we reach the water."

He smiled. "You're just scared of losing to me."

Down at the shoreline, the frothy waves rolled over my feet and sent a chill through me. The Atlantic was colder than I expected, and I dug my toes deeper into the sand, blanketing my feet and cementing myself into the earth. Jim let go of my hand and ran into the water, diving into a wave. A moment later, he stood up and waved me in. I wriggled my feet loose and ran to him, letting his strong arms wrap around me as he began to carry me along with the waves. Under the deep sapphire water, I allowed him to discover every crevice of my body while I explored his. We drifted in the water until we heard the lifeguard's whistle call us back between the flags on the beach that made some imaginary boundary in the water. I glanced down at my wrinkled fingertips.

"Do you want to head in? I'm starting to feel like a raisin."

Jim moved closer, drawing his arms around me and softly caressing the side of my neck with his lips. "Yeah, let's. I'm getting hungry. I might need something beyond the taste of your suntan lotion and salt water."

"Me too. Maybe we start by adding a little tequila and lemon to all this salt."

"Along with a few thousand fish tacos."

He smiled and took my hand as we drew our wet bodies from the ocean. When we reached our blanket, I watched him rifle through the cooler for a glistening can of beer. Then I turned my head as the elderly couple next to us held hands and walked down to the water. They moved slowly, methodically, without any rush of movement. I tapped Jim and nudged my head in their direction. He looked at the couple and then back at me.

"That'll be us in fifty years," I said, meaning every word.

Then I turned my head toward the family on the other side of us. I watched with greater interest than usual. Their youngest child was only a baby but big enough to sit by himself. He was wearing a white beach hat and sunglasses and was sitting in the shade of a giant rainbow-colored umbrella. He screeched joyously each time he picked up a tiny plastic bucket and knocked it onto the sand. An unconscious smile came over me as I stared.

"What are you smiling at?" Jim asked.

"I don't know. That teeny baby over there is so cute. The whole family...so sweet. I have no idea why I'm smiling. I didn't even know that I was."

"Hmmm..." he said, as his eyes touched mine.

"Yeah, hmmm," I said, thoughtfully.

A few hours after we had washed off the taste of the ocean in a steamy outside shower, we headed toward our favorite take-out restaurant on the main drag. The tan-colored building that housed the best seafood at the Shore was minutes from the cottage we had rented for the week. I recognized the wide patio littered with wooden picnic tables as our car pulled in, and my mouth began to water as my eyes met the giant red lobster that lit up the front window.

"Buttery lobster," I said, raising my eyebrows in anticipation.

"And stuffed clams, and calamari, and crab legs, and whatever else they caught today," Jim added, stepping out of the car and drawing in a deep whiff of the fresh seafood and fried fare that hung in the air.

As we walked toward the front door, we maneuvered through an obstacle course of large families, strollers, and high chairs. An astounding number of young children dashed around with fried shrimp and chicken fingers in their hands, adding to the level of difficulty inherent in the hurdles. After we ordered, we sat down at an empty picnic table that still had the remnants of the previous meal pressed into the wood.

I leaned toward Jim and in a hushed voice asked, "Did we accidentally vacation at some strange, new, children's section of the beach? I feel like that's all I see around us—moms, dads, kids, babies, and everything in between." I gestured to the left and right of us directing Jim's attention to the tables filled with young families.

Jim grinned and shook his head. "I think it's always been like this."

"Really?" I scanned the area around me.

Then I looked more closely at the family seated next to us, being conscious not to stare. A young boy with tousled blonde hair and ketchup stains all over his T-shirt reached across the table and grabbed a french fry in each hand; a young girl in a flowered sundress sat next to him, sipping her drink and clutching a doll whose matted hair gave the impression that it never left her side. An infant in a stroller slept soundly next to his mother, oblivious to the cacophony of conversation all around. I looked back at Jim who was also eyeing our surroundings. His tanned skin looked dark against his tangerine-colored shirt.

"Jim, I think we're the only people here without kids."

"Maybe I should get back in line and order a couple."

"Well, that would be the easy way to do it."

I glanced back at the sleeping baby and felt the first spark of desire for motherhood flare up inside me. It was quick and exciting, like a match lit deep within me. With each passing moment, the burning fire began to consume me. I became more conscious of babies, giggles, and children wielding french fries everywhere we went. My eyes were drawn to the young parents and tots that surrounded us in every direction, and I began to drool over that little family who always managed to be right next to us on the beach. An unconscious smile took hold each time I saw that tiny baby sitting under the shade of his rainbow-colored umbrella.

FINDING BALANCE

AS JIM TURNED our packed car into our driveway after our weeklong get-away, I felt different—like I had figured something out. I hadn't gone to the Shore questioning anything or feeling confused. But something had shifted inside me, and I understood the new direction. The dance toward motherhood had begun, and like the tango, the placement of my next step was already a given. I opened the car door and readily stepped into the fresh air. As I stretched my legs, the fragrance of sweet summer roses drifted to my nose.

"It's great to be home and out of the car," I said, extending my arms overhead. "And these flowers smell so great. Remember the girl smelling the roses outside of that pizza place?"

"Yeah, her dad had a cool Yankees T-shirt on. I thought she was going to fall into that rose bush before he scooped her up."

"Luckily he had quick hands."

"Just like the Yanks." Jim popped open the trunk and unloaded our heaviest suitcase. "Here," he said, tilting his chin toward me.

"I'll take the next one, big guy, or maybe we head back to Jersey and grab that dad who always carried so much stuff to the beach. I'm sure he could get everything inside in one trip."

"I bet he could. Can you believe how much stuff he carried each day? Jesus. That family had a thousand things—and they only had one baby."

"I know. I don't know how he managed everything. At one point, I almost felt like they were following us. No matter where I dropped our blanket, they were always on one side of us."

Was that really the case? I wondered. Or would I have been drawn to them wherever they were on the beach—like I was drawn to every other young family everywhere we went? Jim lifted another piece of luggage from the trunk while my mind remained absorbed in thoughts of the sunscreen-soaked child and his doting parents; they had everything for him and attended to his needs like he was the sole customer in a family-owned restaurant.

Jim and I, on the other hand, had only focused on each other and the romance that came seemingly effortlessly—gentle caresses under the ocean water, quiet strolls on the beach, and loving gazes that said more than mere words. At home, the romance came just as easily—unexpected candlelit dinners, sexy sticky-notes left on doors, flowers just because. I realized the spotlight would change if we headed toward parenthood, and I was unsure whether Jim was ready to take the next step. I grabbed my striped beach bag from the back of the car and turned toward him.

"So, I was thinking…" I said, hesitating for a moment. "What do you think about starting a family soon? I think all those babies around us on vacation got to me—or maybe there was something in the water."

A smile took hold of the edges of Jim's mouth, and he approached; his eyes locked with mine. He put his hands on my waist and, without hesitation, said, "Oh yeah, completely ready. And I'm going to enjoy the ride."

"Me too," I whispered. I wrapped my arms around him, embracing a union that went beyond our bodies.

As we carried the remaining bags into the house, I felt my heart explode with excitement. The vivid picture began taking shape in my mind...a rainbow-colored umbrella, teeny sunglasses, plastic shovels and buckets, sand castles, and our own tiny baby. I couldn't wait to start making this vision a reality.

I ran to our bedroom, grabbed my sexiest black bra and thong from my dresser, and raced to the bathroom. I stepped onto the cold tiled floor, quickly changed, and slid back into our bedroom, unnoticed by Jim who was busy unpacking. I slinked behind him and drew my hands under his arms, slowly snaking them onto his chest. He turned around slowly and brought his lips to mine. We made love moments later.

In the midst of our passion, I felt an added intention arise. We weren't together for just the mere pleasure of the dance anymore or for the expression of emotion. Our union had deeper meaning; it held potential like a seed in a freshly planted garden. We were becoming one with the intention of making another. We held each other afterward without uttering a sound. Then I broke the silence.

"Can you imagine if I'm pregnant already?"

"That'd be wild. We'd need to make a few changes around here pretty damn quick—like getting a crib, diapers, a high chair...and some ear plugs."

"What?"

"Yup, ear plugs and maybe a nanny for night duty."

I tried to squirm away, only to find his hold around me tightening. "Somehow, I don't think *that's* going to happen," I laughed.

"We'll see. The Brady's really seemed to dig having Alice around." He chuckled as he hummed a few bars of *The Brady Bunch* theme song and began to kiss my neck. As he brought his lips to my ear, he whispered, "I love you."

"I love you, too," I said, tenderly, feeling closer to him than ever before.

FINDING BALANCE

THE ALARM RANG EARLY in our dark bedroom on Monday morning. The blinds were shut tightly, only a thread of sunlight creeping in, offering an easy invitation to hit the snooze button a few thousand times. Jim and I were clearly still in vacation mode as we slowly crawled out of our warm sheets and started getting ready for work. Even though I was still tired, my insides were brimming with excitement about our new plans.

Jim was out of the bathroom and dressed for work before I had even moved toward a hot shower. I was rifling through my drawers, deciding what to wear, when he walked back into the bedroom with a steaming cup of coffee in hand for me.

"Jesus, I didn't realize how late it is," he groaned, passing the mug over.

As I looked up at him, I noticed how his muscles filled out his tight T-shirt and jeans. Then I glanced at the clock on our dresser. "Shit. You'd better hurry or you're going to get your ass kicked."

"I know. First day back from vacation, and I'm already late." Jim grabbed his beat-up Timex watch from the dresser and buckled it onto his wrist. He walked over to me and kissed me goodbye. "See you later, mama-to-be-someday."

"See you later, daddy-to-be-someday," I beamed.

I sipped my hot coffee and finished getting ready for work, feeling my heart race every time my mind slipped into the prospect of being pregnant. Our lives would be so different, and everything would change so fast—our home, vacations, work. Would I still want a career? I hadn't even thought about it before. I had just assumed that I would, but now, I was beginning to feel differently. I wasn't sure.

Then my mind flooded with all of the other issues and decisions that would arise with a child—breast feeding, bottle feeding, day care, school, religion, God. Immediately, my mind stopped and held on to the profound subject of God, and I began to anguish. Except for the occasional holiday, Jim and I spent most Sundays in bed. All of a sudden, I felt totally unprepared to be a mom. My excitement about parenthood turned into anxiety as a huge knot formed in my stomach. Perspiration ran through me, and I felt my blouse begin to stick to my body. Within minutes, I felt like I needed another shower, and I hadn't even stepped into the New York summer sun.

All day at work my mind was distracted with thoughts of the myriad responsibilities that surround raising a child. I felt over-whelmed, like I had just decided to embark on this massive trip, but I didn't have any sense of direction, or a map, or a car, or a plane ticket, or clothes, or shoes, or money, or any sort of clue. I was beginning to realize the magnitude of this parenting decision beyond the longing feeling in my heart, and I became caught in a tornado of swirling thoughts.

When five o'clock came, I sped home, zipped inside, and waited for Jim in the kitchen. Sitting at the square table that filled the center of the room, I watched the arms of the clock slowly circle the frame. My stomach growled, but the thought of dinner was miles away. I brushed the plaid curtains aside, peered out the window, and felt myself begin to thirst for a beer. But what if I'm pregnant? *Jesus—what if I'm pregnant already?* I walked to the faucet and filled a glass of water. A moment later, I heard Jim's pickup truck pull into the driveway. I turned and watched the door knob turn, pouncing as soon as I saw his dry, muddy boots step inside.

"Jim, I've been thinking about things all day. I really don't know if we're ready for this whole baby thing. I feel like we might need to step back and figure a few things out before we move forward with all this."

"First, hello to you, too. And, second, what do you mean, *before* we move forward? We've already moved forward. We already started trying to have a baby. For all we know, you could be pregnant right now." He walked to the sink and placed his travel mug down, his eyes remaining with mine.

"I know. But today, I was thinking…there are so many things we don't know, so many things we never even thought about— things that a newborn would force us to consider."

"Okay, like what?" he asked incredulously.

"Like breast feeding or bottle feeding, like work and daycare, like religion and God. Jim, we don't even go to church, and I really don't know how I'd feel about getting our child christened in one…making all those promises. Besides deciding on a name and the whole baby food thing, I think that'd be one of the first decisions we'd have to make." I brought my hand to my forehead and pushed back my long, brown hair. I felt tiny beads of perspiration begin to form around my hairline.

"Slow down. We're not the first people we know to have babies. We'll ask around. We'll find out what other people did and what worked, and we'll try that."

"For some things, that'll suffice. But the whole christening thing is huge, and we can't just ask around or read a book or whatever. We need to figure out what feels right for us. We can't go making promises that we're going to raise our kid one way and then not do that, not if we don't really know what we believe in the first place." I looked toward the door, then back at him. "I've already done enough on the road toward raking coals down south. I don't need to throw any more fuel on that fire."

Jim smiled and walked toward me, placing his hands firmly on my shoulders. "Look, I'm going to be your partner raking coals after we've kicked the bucket, just the same. But I hear you. You're right. We should probably check into some stuff. And I think *you* really need to go figure out what you believe in." He squeezed my shoulders, adding, "I guess that whole Catholic upbringing didn't burn itself into your soul then."

I smiled. "I guess not. That's probably why my parents let me leave Catholic school after the ninth grade."

"Or you would've been kicked out?"

"Or the school would've been struck by lightning."

"Gotcha," he laughed.

"You know, you may want to rethink this whole baby thing with me if I'm not pregnant already. My parents used to say, 'I hope your kids are just like you' each time they grounded me for life. In other words, I'm screwed, no matter what."

Jim grinned as he drew me close. "Remember, I fell in love with you during all of those lifetime groundings, and I'm pretty sure my parents said the same thing to me too, so we're both screwed. And come to think of it, there's no one else I'd rather be screwed with or screw." He looked deep into my eyes. "All joking aside, I don't think we'll have all the answers by the time we become parents, but if you feel like you need to do some soul-searching, you'd better do it. I think it'll be worthwhile for you and for our future family."

I nodded and hugged him. He understood. Thank God. The thought of new life in our family had me questioning life at its deepest roots, and the not-so-easy questions would undoubtedly take time to decipher. Jim sauntered into the laundry room to take off his muddy boots as I began to wonder where I would begin my search.

FINDING BALANCE

I SAT DOWN at my desk at work the next day and pulled out a thick phonebook from a squeaky metal drawer. I rustled through the pages, searching for the numbers of local Baptist churches. Recalling how the joyous singing moved people, I had decided to start my search there, knowing if the music or anything else inspired me, I would dig deeper.

I scanned the list of holy places on the yellow page in front of me until my boss, Carol, unexpectedly walked up to my desk, filling the air around me with the fragrance of delicious summer flowers. Carol was a stylish woman in her mid-fifties, and the jewel tones in her blouse made her spirited, hazel eyes pop. She adjusted the jade-colored scarf hanging around her neck and ran her fingers through her short, auburn hair.

"I'm going to head over to the conference. Do you want to catch a ride?"

"Sure," I said, closing the phonebook quickly. "The workshops today should be great."

"I thought the same thing. The planning group worked hard to get speakers from a variety of areas—yoga, tai chi, massage therapy. I didn't realize how many things are out there to relieve stress."

hing."

                        door inset with
                       ctorian house on
                       ooked around the
                       floor under our feet
                       velvety couches and
                       ght musty smell hung
                       r the perfect setting for
                       how to unwind and relax:
                       the backdrop of a bygone

                     r bag and retrieved a stack of
                  ese?"
               over there?" Carol replied, pointing to a table
         center of the room.

I walked over, fanned out the material, and picked up a conference brochure from the corner, skimming over the list of workshops that Carol had begun mentioning earlier. A workshop on meditation immediately caught my eye. I still felt anxious about all of the unknown territory motherhood would bring, and I wondered if meditation could soothe my mind.

"Carol, could I introduce the speaker for the meditation workshop?" I asked, hoping to gain easy access to the session.

"Sure. That would be a big help. Maybe you should check to see if the presenter is already here."

I made my way down a hallway lined with sketches of red brick buildings that once bustled with doctors and patients nearby. Then I walked into a bright, spacious room. Large windows on three sides invited the sunlight in, reflecting the multitude of scratches on the neglected wooden floor.

The guest speaker was leaning against a table, thoughtfully reading over some notes. She appeared to be in her forties with short, cocoa-colored hair and thin-framed glasses. She was wearing a silky, white blouse and loose flowing pants, and I hoped that her relaxed appearance was an indication of the tone of her workshop. I walked over to her and held out my hand.

"Hi, I'm Kelly. I'll be introducing you today."

"Hi. Nice to meet you. I'm Kathy. I really don't need a big introduction. After you say my name, I'll take it from there, if that's okay."

"Sure. That makes my job a lot easier. I'll stay for the rest of the workshop in case you need anything," I added, aware that my real intention for staying stemmed from my desire to hear more about meditation and anything else that might ease my raft into the river of parenthood.

Kathy stepped away and began to arrange the chairs around us into a semicircle. After the audience arrived and took their seats, I introduced her. She strolled easefully to the front of the room to begin her own introduction.

"Welcome everyone. You may have come here to learn how to calm your mind or to relax, or maybe for some other health or spiritual reason. The beautiful thing about meditation is that it has a natural way of touching on all of those aspects. Many find that while they come to meditation for a specific purpose, they also feel its benefits in other areas of their life. I can attest to that. Let me tell you a little bit about myself and how my journey led me to meditation, and then we'll meditate together.

"There was a time in my life when I felt like I had everything on the outside—a loving husband, three healthy kids, a beautiful home, nice clothes, everything. But inside, I felt like something was missing—missing on a more spiritual level. Although I was raised in a Jewish home, I studied different religious paths. All of my studies and spiritual experiences ultimately led me to my guru. He taught me about meditation, chanting, and God from a yogic perspective, and I found my missing piece."

Did Kathy just say guru? I wondered, feeling my curiosity grow. My limited perception of meditation began to expand beyond the image of a person sitting effortlessly on the floor, legs crossed, eyes closed. I leaned toward Kathy, eager to hear more.

"Meditation was one of the keys that allowed me to find the stillness within, even when things around me were everything but that. It quieted my mind and let me touch something deeper inside. I initially came to meditation for spiritual reasons, but I also benefitted from a calmer physical and mental state. You can choose to simply enjoy the practice itself or you can study it more deeply. As you may have gathered, I chose to dive a little deeper."

Kathy picked up a stack of business-sized cards and handed one to each person, explaining that the words written on them, *Om Namah Shivaya*, were a mantra first shared by yogis thousands of years ago. "The words on the card mean 'I bow to, or honor, Shiva.' In other words, I bow to, or honor, God, the divinity that resides within me and everything. Chanting a mantra can bring your mind into single focus to get it ready for meditation." She pressed the play button on a tape recorder, and the voices of people slowly singing the mantra resounded throughout the room.

I looked down at the card in my hands and realized that I had never considered preparing my mind to do anything. Sure, I had prepared things for dinner or a road trip, but I had always assumed that my mind didn't need any readying. It went where it needed to go—usually where I directed it—and its wanderings were just part of its nature.

"Just listen to the words, the sounds of the mantra. Let them envelop you. If you feel comfortable, close your eyes and join in the singing without a care about how you sound or anyone around you."

Kathy began to chant along with the tape. Soon thereafter, I joined her, quietly at first. My eyes remained focused on the card. When I had the hang of the words, I closed my eyes and allowed myself to sing without a thought of the people nearby. My heart sang along with my voice as we chanted *Om Namah Shivaya*. Even though my voice sang the words out loud, an inner stillness began to reside within me. My mind didn't flash from one thought to the next. It remained with the mantra. Then even the mantra seemed to disappear like the subtle exit of elevator music in conversation. It fell below any conscious stream of thought. For a moment, nothing else existed but the quietness of my mind, the stillness within me. And then, without notice, my mind stirred and returned to the mantra, and I realized I was singing again.

Was I singing out loud like this? Saying part of the mantra and then nothing? I wasn't sure. During that feeling of nothingness, of no thoughts, I experienced such peaceful stillness. I couldn't recall ever feeling that serene before; thoughts were usually my constant companion. After some time, Kathy slowly turned down the music, and the room fell silent.

"Keep your eyes closed if they already are or close them and say those words silently to yourself with each inhalation and exhalation. *Om Namah Shivaya* as you breathe in and *Om Namah Shivaya* as you breathe out."

We meditated. I was captivated. I heard the jingle of a tiny bell, and Kathy asked us to slowly open our eyes. I had no idea how long we had been sitting there—chanting, meditating, becoming still—and I had lost any sense of my role in this workshop as an aid to the speaker. I was only there now as a workshop participant, a member of the audience entranced by this introduction to meditation.

"When your mind comes to that place of stillness," Kathy whispered, "your whole being is calmed. As you may have just realized, meditation can bring you there." She picked up a stack of papers and began to distribute them. "My guru died years ago, but he passed the torch, so to say, to a special swami, a monk, who will be visiting my house this weekend for a little get-together.

If you're interested in chanting and meditating as we did today, you're welcome to join us. Just follow the directions on the flyer."

A guru…a swami…I was intrigued. These words were so foreign to me. The only time that I had used the word *guru* was in reference to whoever could get the coffee pot at work to turn on. I tucked the flyer into my pocketbook and looked down again at the small card that Kathy had given to us. I stared at the words *Om Namah Shivaya* printed on one side and realized that the translation was printed on the other side. The words seemed to hold some magical power to bring a stop to my incessant thinking. I wondered if I said the word *abracadabra* quietly to myself, in the same manner, whether it would work just the same? I smiled as I buried the card alongside the flyer.

The next day at work, I dug into my pocketbook and retrieved the card. As I stared at the mantra, I couldn't recall ever reading anything so beautiful or unusual before. Somehow I wanted more of it.

I picked up a folder from the corner of my desk and slid the card into it. I sprinted down the hallway, removed it inconspicuously, and carefully centered it on top of a copier. I enlarged the image so that it met the edges of an 8.5 by 11 inch piece of paper and returned to my desk. Then I hung the magnified mantra on a wall in front of me. It immediately gave an international feel to my cubby, like the spicy aroma of chicken curry or tikka masala sauce. As I stared at it, I realized it offered me the opportunity to share more creative translations of its meaning with anyone who might ask.

"Yes, I'm sure," I stated adamantly to a coworker, moments later. "It means 'All beer ultimately comes from God'—in Sanskrit."

To another, I found myself saying, "Look it up. It means 'Every day should be a vacation day.' If we were wise, we'd follow that ancient advice and head out now. Give me five minutes and I'll meet you at my car."

It's not surprising that I felt the burning flames of the afterlife lick my heels on a regular basis.

FINDING BALANCE

THE FOLLOWING SATURDAY, I looked down at the flyer that Kathy had handed out in her workshop. I felt excitement grab hold of me as I anticipated exploring something that might help me firm up my spiritual foundation and relieve some of the pre-parent anxiety coursing through my veins. I rummaged through my closet, wondering what I might wear to a gig showcasing a guru. I finally settled on a pair of khaki capris and a short sleeve top—something I recently wore out with friends, where a nice pinot grigio accompanied some fettuccini. Jim was already at work and was aware of my plan to head to Kathy's house.

"Just go ahead without me," he had said after I asked him to join me. "Let me know if you find what you're looking for."

I smiled as I recalled his words. *Let's hope I do*, I thought.

Then my mind turned to the upcoming program and the clouds that surrounded it. Would Kathy's guru do things differently than she did? Would he read, or talk, or sing, or chant, or make a nice minestrone soup incorporating everything? I felt a pang of nervousness run through me as I realized I wasn't sure of anything, except for my desire to give this visit a shot.

A short while later, I followed the rich, dark-brown wooden

fences lining the sides of Kathy's long driveway and continuing around lush pastures where black and brown horses grazed. I parked behind a line of cars and walked toward an old, white farmhouse at the end, feeling as if I should be shopping for homemade jam or fresh pies in this country setting rather than meeting some sort of guru.

I walked onto Kathy's porch and noticed that it was lined with wooden shelves filled with people's shoes. I removed mine, opened the front door, and walked inside. The smoky scent of incense hung in the air, and I readily joined about forty other people sitting on pillows on the floor. Most were sitting quietly, some whispering to another. They were of varying ages, from their twenties to their seventies, and dressed casually. As I scanned the room for Kathy, my eyes inadvertently met those of the other guests. Their expressions were friendly and hospitable, immediately making me feel welcome, and I began to feel as if I was at a neighborhood block party where I didn't know anyone well but felt like I belonged.

The room itself seemed like a normal living room with a brown, upholstered couch lining one wall. Framed pictures of horses and members of Kathy's family, I assumed, hung on the cream-colored walls around us. As I eyed the photos more closely, I noticed that some were of a darker-skinned man wearing an orange knit hat. His picture was often taken with his hands together in front of his heart as if he was praying. I began to wonder whether the picture was of Kathy's father or of her guru, the one who had died.

As another guest arrived, I shifted my gaze to the front door and noticed a wooden sign hanging above it inscribed with the mantra *Om Namah Shivaya*. Then I looked toward the far end of the room. A man likely in his mid-thirties sat on a large, tangerine-colored cushion. He was sporting an orange short-sleeve shirt and matching wrap around his legs. His darker complexion, onyx-colored hair, and short black beard gave the impression that he was possibly of Indian or Middle Eastern descent. Coupled with the burning incense, his presence gave an international feel to the gathering. I assumed that he was Kathy's teacher.

A few moments later, Kathy walked into the room. She walked over and leaned down toward me.

"So glad you could make it. The program is just about to start."

"Great, thanks for inviting me."

My mind was busy taking in the new scenery and was miles away from the quiet space it had rested in during her meditation workshop. Kathy walked over to the man dressed in orange, her teacher, and publicly welcomed him. She referred to him as *Guruji*, a customary term of respect that she had referenced in her workshop and compared to the word "father" when it is used in reference to a priest.

A few moments later, a young woman began playing music on an old fashioned-looking instrument that sat on the ground directly in front of her. The piece was only a couple of feet wide, maybe a foot high, and looked like a mix between an accordion and a mini piano. As the woman touched the black and white keys, deep, mellow notes floated into the air, held for long moments when she fanned out the accordion-like section. The wooden instrument made the same sounds that I had heard in Kathy's workshop when she had played the mantra on the tape. Kathy had called the instrument behind the music a harmonium.

Soon, the crowd began to sing. The words weren't in English and were different from the mantra I had chanted at Kathy's meditation workshop. I looked around and noticed that the resounding words were displayed on a poster on a wall nearby. I stared at them for a moment and listened to the way they were supposed to be pronounced. Then I joined in. Although I didn't understand their meaning, I enjoyed the rhythm and the way they brought me to a space of relaxation and focus. As I sang, I melted into the room. The chanting started out really slow, then grew faster and faster, and then slowed down again. I loved the movement of the chant; it reminded me of the waves of the ocean.

Once the chant ended, we sat in silence and meditated. I used the ancient key that Kathy shared in her workshop to bring my mind back into focus when everyday thoughts arose. *Om Namah Shivaya* began to flow with my breath, and I relished the peaceful space that I sat in. The quiet space was only interrupted when the harmonium began to sound again, and the man introduced as Guruji began a brief, slow chant. When I opened my eyes, I glanced around and found that most people were already staring at Guruji.

With his hands together in front of his chest, he said, "With great respect and love, I welcome you." Then he began speaking about the importance of becoming quiet within and getting in touch with something deeper, something that resides within each of us. The space he created invited stillness of mind and a unity among all people. I embraced his thoughtful words and the openness of his message. I felt as if I was being hugged—from the inside out—and when the program ended, I found myself wanting more.

I drove home as if my car was on autopilot. While I stopped at every red light and stayed marginally close to the speed limits, my mind and heart remained captivated with Guruji's universal message. I felt like I was heading in the right direction in my spiritual quest, and I couldn't wait to get home to share the experience with Jim.

"Well, it was great," I exclaimed before I had both feet in the house.

"So you've found your yellow brick road?" Jim asked.

"Yeah, maybe. I'm still looking for my ruby slippers, but I enjoyed meeting all of the people at Kathy's—in the Land of Oz. And honestly, I think that you'd dig it, too—maybe not the singing so much but everything that was said. It just makes so much sense. It seems to cross all faiths."

"What do you mean?"

"I don't know. The guy who was there, the guru, Guruji..."

"Wait—the guru? A guru was there? Do you think a guru would really fly in a Jewish or Christian religion? What are you saying?"

"No, I know. It sounds crazy, but I really think that everything he said ties into those religions. Guruji talked about the unity among everyone, that same inner-something that joins us together. It's not about this one path or that one path. It's just about finding that source within you. I only got a taste of it, but I want to learn more. Kathy is offering a four-week "Learn to Meditate" class at her house in a couple of weeks, and I think I want to go."

"So do it. And in the meantime, let's keep trying to make a baby." Jim pulled me into his chest and kissed me seductively on the mouth. A moment later, he took my hand in his and led me into our bedroom.

The next day, we woke up in one another's arms. After I shut the alarm clock off, I walked to the bathroom with my eyes half open. A moment later, I realized I had gotten my period. A wave of sadness and disappointment washed over me. Even though I had only just begun mentally preparing to be a mother and even felt some trepidation, my heart was ready to take hold of a new life.

I trudged back to the bedroom where Jim was already dressing for work. After he tucked his bright orange shirt into his pants, he looked over at me, and I frowned.

"Well, there's no rushing out to get diapers yet. I just got my damn period."

"That's okay," he said, walking over to hug me. "I'm enjoying the 'trying to have a baby' part. We'll keep trying. It will happen. I know it. I guess we just need more practice." He offered a slight smile and winked at me.

I didn't feel like smiling or winking. I felt like crying. I wanted to take the next step and was beginning to feel a lack of control in becoming pregnant. I tried to console myself by keeping in mind that we had just started trying to get pregnant, and I wasn't even prepared to raise a child yet. I was still figuring things out. But inside, I still felt a deep longing and lack of patience...like the kind you begin to feel a few days before Christmas—when you're seven.

A COUPLE OF WEEKS LATER, I found myself again following the dark, rich fences that outlined lush green meadows and led to Kathy's house. I had signed up for her four-week "Learn to Meditate" course, but this time I brought two friends with me, Donna and Colleen. They were sisters and were the friends you would ask to help bury a body, search for UFOs, or attend a four-week meditation course. They would do anything with me. Although Donna was older than Colleen, they could almost pass as twins. Their hair was the same: short, blonde, highlighted, chic. Their mannerisms were the same. They even laughed alike.

"Jesus, Kelly. Are you taking us to some dude ranch or something?" Donna joked, as she stepped out of the car onto the stone driveway, admiring the pastures.

"Yes, Donna. Surprise. Here we are. Your cowboy boots are in the trunk." I rolled my eyes, adding, "This place is gorgeous, but Kathy won't let you move in even if you try wrangling up all of her horses."

"We'll see, Tonto."

Colleen and I exchanged smiles, as we walked toward Kathy's porch. I turned back around and gazed beyond the green fields, drawing in a deep breath of freshly cut grass. As I walked through Kathy's doorway and the scent of incense replaced the fragrance of the outdoors, I felt a more serious tone come over me. I chose to sit as far away from my friends as possible, hoping to concentrate on the meditation course itself and not on the next sarcastic jab. I knew that I wouldn't be able to listen to Kathy, or allow myself to find the stillness I had felt at her previous gatherings, unless I put some space between my friends and me—and even this plan wasn't a sure thing. Since there were only five people in the class, I was only able to move as far away from them as the opposite side of the couch.

As I sank into the cushion, Colleen looked over at me and mouthed, "Do I smell?"

I mouthed back, "Yes, as usual."

Colleen nodded and laughed, realizing I had just given her some great material for the car ride home.

A moment later, Kathy walked into her living room and informally introduced herself to my friends. Then she stepped to the front of the class and began speaking more about mantras, chanting, meditation, and her guru. The class inspired a deeper level of conversation and reflection than anything I had experienced in a workshop before as Kathy allowed our conversations to follow tangents under the larger umbrella of meditation and spirituality. She posed profound questions to the class and encouraged us to look within ourselves for answers.

I began to contemplate transcendental subjects as I had never done before. What is my true nature? What exists beyond this body? What happens to my sense of "self" when I meditate? Where does my mind go? Why are we here? The questions felt huge in my heart and mind, opening up deep feelings of connection to humanity and unearthing a multitude of questions relative to my existence. Regardless of religion, I knew that people everywhere asked these same questions, and in some way,

I felt a union with them in the search for answers. My view of my very existence expanded, and I felt a communion with people stretching across oceans as I began to realize and appreciate the notion of a greater force in the universe ultimately linking us all together.

Kathy began peppering our discussion with insight from ancient yogic sages who seemed to provide a compass for the hills and valleys of my mind. Their understanding of the universe and the tools they offered to quiet the mind, like meditation, helped to lift some of the cloudiness within—but I knew that it was up to me to choose the path that resonated truth. Nothing was black or white for me anymore, and oddly, I didn't feel confused. I felt inspired to reflect further. One question led to another with seemingly infinite right answers, and I realized this study of me would take time—maybe more than these short workshops could offer.

"The understanding that you gain from these great teachers and discussions comes from your own contemplation of these subjects beyond the walls of my living room," Kathy shared. "Meditate. Sit and allow your mind to grow quiet, and you will get in touch with a deeper understanding of yourself. At each class together, we will look further into meditation and touch on other related subjects."

While I had been captivated by every topic of discussion throughout the evening, my friends had remained less enthused. Although they enjoyed our time with Kathy, the information was not brand new to them. They had taken meditation classes before and had even tried their hand at chanting but were never big fans of it. Clearly, their excitement didn't mirror mine.

I wanted to remain entrenched in the ethereal topics that we had begun discussing and allow them to lead me to a deeper understanding of myself and the powers of the universe. The wisdom of the sages and insight from this workshop resonated with something in my heart. And although the discourse was new to me, I felt like the answers were buried treasure within me, and I had just gotten my hands on the treasure map. I didn't want the class to end.

When I picked up my friends for the next session, they were aware that I was taking the subject seriously and that the car ride there and back was our only opportunity to bust each other's chops. Since our banter flowed with the ease of an Abbott and Costello routine, there was never a lull in the conversation. Who was always on first. What was on second and I Don't Know was on third. We were bursting with laughter by the time my car pulled down Kathy's driveway.

As she shut the car door, Colleen roared, "So, really, try NOT to think of the time you laughed so hard, orange soda shot out of your nose, Kelly, when Kathy says, 'Close your eyes and say the mantra to yourself.' You know that your real mantra has always been the sound of orange soda climbing through your nostrils."

"Some other mantras are quickly coming to mind, Colleen—just for you. But if I think of orange soda later, you'll be walking home."

"I will be until I round up one of Kathy's horses. I'm fine bareback."

"I've heard that about you. I think I may have read it on a bathroom wall somewhere."

I was still smiling as I bent down and removed my shoes. Then I reached for the door, hoping that the threshold to Kathy's house would bathe me in serenity. As I entered her home, I breathed in the familiar fragrance of patchouli. I looked at the sign above my head. *Om Namah Shivaya.* As my mind flitted back to orange soda, I looked over at Colleen and shook my head, and she returned a quick wink.

Once Kathy entered the room, she brought all of our thoughts and discussion to meditation. We examined different ways to draw the mind into single-pointed focus so that meditation could come more readily. I had never realized the flurry of thoughts constantly running through my head until I tried to sit quietly.

"Let's chant *Om Namah Shivaya* together," Kathy offered.

I closed my eyes. As we chanted, my mind remained with the mantra, and no other thoughts crept in—not even orange soda. I felt comfortable, as if I was singing a sweet, familiar song; I no longer had to look at the words on a card or a poster, or even concentrate on the words themselves. They were tucked away in an easily accessible compartment of my mind, like the theme song from a favorite TV show or an often-heard lullaby.

For some time after we stopped chanting and sat in silence, my mind remained focused on the mantra. Then, without notice, my mind bounced to the deep spiritual questions that I hoped we would discuss later in class. My mind let go of the easy repetition of the mantra and began to question where it originally came from and why it soothed my mind so easily.

As Kathy began to chant the mantra aloud again, I heard the soft union of our voices. I opened my eyes slowly and raised my hand with my first question.

Kathy nodded her head in understanding and replied, "Kelly, all mantras ultimately come from the Absolute, from God. Many are found in ancient texts, while some have been given verbally from guru to disciple. Mantras often evoke a communion, or a feeling, within us—one that goes beyond their mere sounds."

"Thank you," I replied.

One question down, only a million to go.

Time at Kathy's workshops flew by. Before I knew it, I was

sitting in her living room in the final class. As I gazed around the room, I realized how familiar the space had become—the pictures, the couch, even the incense. The ashy smell and homey surroundings had become rich parts of the cocoon of our discussions.

"I've enjoyed getting to know each of you these last four weeks," Kathy shared. "I hope that this meditation course met your expectations and sparked a desire within you to meditate."

I smiled to myself knowing that my desire to learn more about God, meditation, mantras, and even gurus had grown.

"Each week, I offer a one-hour meditation session at my house," she continued. "We do some chanting. Then I share some insight from a spiritual book, and we meditate. If you'd like to join me and a few others, you are more than welcome. We meet every Thursday evening."

Perfect, I thought. My study here could continue. Since I had first heard the mantra, *Om Namah Shivaya,* in Kathy's initial workshop, something inside me was drawn to it. Its repetition made me feel as if I was dialing up God, and throughout Kathy's classes, it offered me a deep sense of peace. All of the discussions in class and the ponderings afterward also affirmed my connection to the yogic teachings on this path. I still had so many questions, but I felt as if I was moving in the right direction, closer to the giant X on the treasure map and possibly down the spiritual road that I longed for—one that I could share with Jim and a future family.

The following Thursday, I headed to Kathy's horse farm again, only this time alone. While I drove toward greener pastures, Donna and Colleen headed in a different direction. My car ride there was a lot quieter, and it lacked the boisterous laughter, but

I held on to the same enthusiasm.

As I walked into Kathy's living room, I smiled as I recognized some of the people from Guruji's visit. They looked like your average Joe and Joann; nothing stood out in their appearances. Some were dressed in business clothes like they had just stepped out of the office, while others donned more casual attire like they were headed to a friend's house for a few glasses of chardonnay. The small audience was seated on pillows on the floor. Kathy greeted me cheerfully and reintroduced me to the handful of others in the room. Then she sat down on the floor behind the musical instrument that I had grown accustomed to seeing and hearing and began to play some low-pitched notes on the harmonium.

I closed my eyes. A few moments later, Kathy started chanting the words *Hare Ram, Hare Krishna*. Immediately, my mind zipped to a picture of the bald, flower-peddling Hare Krishnas that floated around the airports in the '70s, and my heart started beating the rhythm of a fast tango. *Is this what I'm getting into? Hare Krishnas?* I gasped. I was still so new to meditation; maybe I was also naïve. I wanted to raise my hand and ask Kathy about any connection here, but after the chant ended, we moved straight into a different discussion.

Kathy handed out notes on the book *The Sermon on the Mount According to Vedanta* by Swami Prabhavananda. The book focused on the similarities between the teachings of Jesus and Vedanta, the philosophical backbone of Hinduism. Without delay, she began a discussion around some of the shared tenets from each path. As I gazed over the notes, I convinced myself that this couldn't be the Hare Krishnas from the airport. Although I wasn't one hundred percent sure, I didn't think that I would be comparing teachings from Christianity and Hinduism in such a gathering, and Kathy probably would have been bald. Her hair looked too real. After the meditation program ended, I approached her.

"So, Kathy, what would you say these teachings fall under? Like what religious or spiritual umbrella?"

Please don't say Hare Krishnas, I silently begged the universe.

"It's yoga, Kelly. Real yoga—not just the physical yoga you may be familiar with. This particular tradition falls under the umbrella of Hinduism, and there are even finer threads within that context. I can lend you some books written by some amazing teachers that will shed some light on where all of this comes from, if you want. The roots of these yogic traditions are deep and very, very old."

Oh, thank God, I thought, heaving a sigh of relief. No need to shave my head or pass out flowers anytime soon.

"Okay, great," I replied, elated. "I definitely want to learn more. I'd love to borrow some books. Thank you."

I wanted to learn as much as I could to ensure that I was heading down a path that was right for me and any possible future family that Jim and I might be starting, especially as I realized how little I knew about any of this.

I devoured the books that Kathy lent me. The first book that I read was *Where Are You Going? A Guide to the Spiritual Journey* by Swami Muktananda. The title itself seemed to perfectly capture the theme of my existence recently and offer the answer that I longed for. The book posed profound vignettes that made me ponder the smallest of things—like how an entire banyan tree can be encapsulated in the tiny seed it grows from—to the larger questions tied to our existence in the universe. I began to thoughtfully consider the complexities of creation as well as the miracle of it all. I was amazed at the creative powers that Jim and I seemingly held in our hands and in our efforts to start a family. My belief in a greater creative force—beyond us—grew, as did my connection to all things around me as I read the same universal questions in Swami Muktananda's book that I longed to have answered in my mind. It affirmed a deep connection within me to all spiritual seekers.

A few weeks later, I found myself saying, "Kathy, I think I'd like to see Guruji again. Is he coming to your house anytime soon?"

"No, nothing is planned right now," Kathy replied. "But as I've mentioned before, he has an ashram half an hour away, and you're welcome to go there anytime. He offers weekend meditation retreats and chanting. I'd be happy to meet you there anytime you want to go."

An ashram? I had no idea what Kathy was referring to. I tried to hide the puzzled look on my face. The word itself sounded so international and mystical to me, like the perfect meeting place for people like Austin Powers—or Gandhi.

"Okay. Let me look into my schedule," I said. "I'll let you know. I think I'd really like to see him again."

I knew that Guruji would be able to tell me more about this path than mere books alone. Somewhere within me, the flame that I felt in Kathy's meditation workshop was being stoked with this new information, and I needed to continue to feed the fire.

FINDING BALANCE

7

WEEKS LATER, I turned my car onto a gravelly road, well off the beaten path. Both sides of the street were lined with forest, except for small openings that had been cut out for long driveways and front yards that provided clearings for cars, families, and roaming deer. I followed one of the driveways straight back to an ordinary two-story house nestled in the woods. My friend and fellow explorer Donna was by my side.

"Not what I expected," I said, somewhat confused.

"Yes, I agree. Not what I expected either."

"I was expecting an ashram to have some domes and colorful statues—maybe even some cobras and belly dancers."

"Yeah, me too," Donna laughed. "The sign doesn't even stand out. It looks so dull and blah."

The ashram's lengthy driveway and expansive front yard offered it some privacy, but other than the drab sign, there wasn't any indication that this was a place for spiritual seekers. We stepped out of the car slowly and began to walk down a short path to the entrance. After we walked through the front door and onto an enclosed porch, we followed the directions on a sign that read "Please Remove Shoes."

We opened another door, immediately smelled incense, and

were transported to a different world altogether. There was no furniture in this room; at the far end was a giant, golden statue of a man sitting cross-legged. The statue sat on a massive marble stand and was flanked by two golden objects that resembled wide candlestick holders with a flame visible on the top of each. Other statues of lesser scale and pictures of wondrous beings with multiple arms adorned the room. I had never seen anything like them before, except maybe in Greek mythology. I looked around for something familiar, like a picture of a flying horse or a gigantic sea creature, but found none.

Kathy came over and greeted us, then led us to two flat, pastel-colored pillows that she had placed on the carpeted floor near her. We sat down among twenty others and waited for the program to begin. As I scanned the crowd, some of the faces were familiar to me from Kathy's meditation get-togethers, and I exchanged smiles with those I recognized. Donna, on the other hand, remained focused on the enormous figure in the front of the room.

Although Donna had gone to Kathy's "Learn to Meditate" class with me, she wasn't a regular at her weekly meditation gigs, and she had come along with me to the ashram with some hesitation. She wasn't fond of chanting words that she didn't understand, and both of us knew that was on the menu. Her fear reminded me of an old movie I'd seen where actors chant witch spells they read from a movie script and don't realize that they are actually waking the dead. I had a bit more faith in the foreign words that we were about to sing, but I understood her trepidation and was glad to have my skeptical, grounded friend with me.

I leaned toward Donna and whispered, "You've got about three seconds left to bolt or you're going to be stuck here for the program."

"I don't even have the keys to your car, Kel, so I think I'm here for the duration."

"The keys are in my shoes on the porch. Just give me a sign if you head out and I need to grab a ride with Kathy or another kind soul."

Donna smiled and rolled her eyes, turning her head toward one of the multi-armed statues in the room.

A few minutes later, a woman in a silky, coral-colored sari entered the room and sat down behind a harmonium. She began to play some slow notes on the instrument to open the chant. I closed my eyes, breathed in the incense, and allowed myself to become immersed. As I sang, I had no idea of the meaning of any of the words, nor did I know whether I was wakening the dead, but I loved it nonetheless. One chant moved right into another, and to my amazement, I found the strange words rolling off my tongue. Somehow, it seemed, the chant was connecting to a deeper melody within me, to a rhythm beyond mere words or sounds, to the rhythm of my soul. I didn't feel as if I was struggling with a foreign language; my mind stepped aside and let my heart sing.

At some point during the chant, Guruji walked in and sat down next to the golden statue in the front of the room. I heard his deep, strong voice join ours as we sang. After the chant ended, we sat in silence for a few minutes. Then Guruji began to chant aloud, and everyone joined in, except for Donna and me. I looked around and had no idea how everyone knew what to say. I didn't see a poster displaying the words being sung nor did I see anyone reading the words from a book. The chant lasted only a few moments, and then the room fell silent again. I watched as Guruji drew his hands together to welcome everyone. He began to talk about the universal essence in all people and the importance of meditation.

At the end of the program, people began to walk up to Guruji and bow. Since many of my college years had been filled with pro-women activist events, I felt my pride cementing me to my pillow.

Kathy leaned toward Donna and me and whispered, "If you'd like to meet him, I'll go up with you. And you don't have to bow in front of Guruji if you don't want to."

Relieved to know that I could meet this swami standing tall, I replied, "Sure. Let's go." I looked over at Donna and she declined, shaking her head as if she had been asked to lead the next chant.

I rose from my pillow and stood in line, wondering whether Guruji would recognize me from his visit to Kathy's house. Then I watched person after person bow in front of him. My mind skirted to all of the talks and discussions I had recently heard or been a part of that centered on the notion of a greater being or divinity residing within each of us. I questioned whether I should bow to that divinity within Guruji—not to the man but to that special something within him. Was that what people were doing when they bowed? All of a sudden, I was there—at the front of the line before Guruji.

Kathy introduced me and I said, "Thank you for all of the wisdom you shared." And almost automatically, without hesitation, I bent down on the carpeted floor and bowed. *I am bowing to the divinity within you, not to the person, but to the God within you*, I said to myself. Although my heart had overcome my mind, I still felt this need to remind myself on the inside.

As I stood up and walked away, I realized that I had been moved by the grace and virtue of his being. Guruji's humility and benevolence had allowed me to open up and let go of my pride for a moment and bow. I was so enthralled and surprised with his tenderness and down-to-earth manner, especially after watching people lay at his feet. Although it was a huge deal in my feminist mind, I was genuinely at ease with my last-minute decision to demonstratively genuflect. Then I wondered what Gloria Steinem would have thought.

When I returned to my seat, Donna smiled at me. Then she

turned her head and checked the door for any signs of the risen dead. After the program ended and Guruji left the room, my friend and I stood up, said goodbye to Kathy, and walked to the car in silence.

Once we shut the car doors, I turned toward Donna and asked, "So, what did you think?"

"Well, you know I'm not really into singing foreign words," she began. "I liked what he said about the universality of things, of God, but I just couldn't get into the singing."

"I understand. I can't explain why, but I really liked it. And I liked that whole talk about the universality of things, too. It reminded me of the book we're discussing at Kathy's, *The Sermon on the Mount According to Vedanta*. So many different religions or paths but so much similarity. It's like with coffee—so you like it black, or with milk, or with cream, or with sugar, or with whatever. It's all just different flavors of the same thing. I feel like spirituality is like coffee, and everyone likes it different ways. You know, Donna, I think I found my cup of coffee."

"Well, I know you like your coffee with sambuca in it sometimes too, and I don't think they're serving that here."

"Yeah, that's true. But it's still coffee—and I can always add my sambuca at home."

Later that day, as I sat alone on my back porch, I noticed that my mind wasn't filled with the chatter of my thoughts. I was beginning to bring the tranquility that I felt at the ashram and Kathy's meditation sessions back home with me. Although the ashram was completely different from the church I went to when I was younger, and I was still a bit hesitant to embrace a path where the language, the programs, the guru were so foreign to me, the teachings had a similar thread running through them; in my heart, I felt the union. I felt a peace that stemmed from something deeper inside me, something I felt in my core.

I started going to the ashram more often, in addition to Kathy's weekly meditation gatherings. I became more familiar with the multi-armed beings in the pictures and held on to the overarching theme of oneness even though I was surrounded by various pictures and statues of gods and goddesses. Their forms were distinct, and they represented diverse qualities or attributes, but they were all parts of the same creative force (or, at least, that's how I understood it).

While I was swimming in all of this spirituality, Jim was busy working and driving a race car at a local racetrack. He spent hours under the hood of a 358 Sportsman stock car, and I spent time under the halo of incense and mystical song. Our lives felt balanced. Both of us were doing things that we wanted to do for ourselves, and we still made time for one another together. I also made time to go to the racetrack and share in Jim's racing world on a few occasions, just as he made time to go to the ashram and share in my spiritual world a few times.

"I can't sit next to you?" I recalled Jim asking before he had made his first trip to the ashram.

"No. Women sit on one side and men on the other, so there's no chance you can get away with trying to make me laugh there."

"We'll see," he had teased.

As I thought back to that first visit, I smiled. I realized that Jim had kept his jokes to himself until we returned home. But now, I wondered. *Had he kept things on the serious side because he was being respectful or did he actually feel something there—or was he on heightened alert because Donna told him about the possibility of zombies walking in while strange and unfamiliar words hung in the air?* It was all still a bit of a mystery to me.

II

CAR SEATS, BABIES, and MARRIAGE IN THE BACK SEAT

FINDING BALANCE

WHILE I REVELED in finding a spiritual path that I grooved with, Jim and I continued to indulge our passion for each other in our attempts to conceive. Both quests had become constants in our lives.

*Jesus! How can this be so difficult? Why can't I get pregnant? I must've been completely crazy to have always been so worried about getting pregnant before…*before I was enamored with tiny sunglasses, little beach hats, and babies playing in the sand. Sex had always come so easily but getting pregnant seemed like trying to find the perfect pair of shoes in a grocery store—just not happening. What could we be doing wrong?

Each time I got my period, I wasn't only annoyed because it was that time of the month; I was disappointed that I wasn't pregnant. I started doing research on things that might increase my chances of getting pregnant.

"Jim, right after we do it, I'm going to lift my ass off the bed and hold it in the air with my hands, keeping my legs in the air."

"Okay," he replied, somewhat bewildered. "How long are you going to stay like that?"

"Probably an hour or so, I guess."

"An hour or so? What?"

"I'm just joking, smart-ass. I think for like five or ten minutes. I heard that gravity will help force your sperm back downstream into my ovaries."

"Okay," he laughed. "Do whatever you think will work."

"Honestly, I don't know if this will work, but I'm going to give it a try. We have nothing to lose."

"Yup. You're right. And I'm looking forward to seeing what you're going to do next. Maybe something a bit more exciting next time—like with a trapeze or some sexy dance moves." He raised his eyebrows and grinned widely.

"Not likely. But I think there may be something you can do after this," I said, as my mind flitted to the article I had read on the relationship between wearing boxers and having a higher sperm count.

I had headed down the road of pre-pregnancy madness. I started calculating the perfect time to have sex and, in so doing, took most of the spontaneity out of our intimate moments. Sex became more of a means to become pregnant rather than a pleasure tour, and I was beginning to feel a teeny cloud of pressure each time we made love, hoping that Jim's sperm would just take hold or that my ovaries would somehow just grab them. Had I found a voodoo spell or magic potion to help quicken the process, I probably would have used it. But sadly, the only thing I had close to international mysticism was the ashram, and it didn't offer any strange potions, only mantras that settled my mind—not my ovaries.

Months later, no thanks to any magical spell or post-sex acrobatics, I stepped out of the bathroom, my glassy eyes meeting Jim's immediately.

"You're going to be a dad," I said, as the sides of my mouth curled up. The plastic pregnancy test stick was still in my hands.

"And you're going to be a mom. I guess we're lucky we moved into a house big enough for a family."

"Just in time."

Jim walked over and hugged me. As I released my hold, I gazed over his shoulder at the empty walls of our new bedroom, spotting the perfect location for pictures of our new baby.

Eight weeks later, I found myself in my obstetrician's office. My doctor had lathered my belly with warm, slimy gel and was gliding an instrument all over it in search of a heartbeat. Jim was by my side, listening intently. I heard a low rushing noise like the ocean and wondered whether that could be the sound that my doctor was in search of. The somber look on her face seemed to say no.

"I'm having some difficulty locating your baby's heartbeat," she said, fixedly. "There's no cause for alarm. I'm just going to send you downstairs for a sonogram where the instruments are stronger and will give us a better picture of what's going on."

"Okay," I replied, apprehensively, feeling Jim cradle my hand in both of his.

I reached for a paper towel and wiped the gel from my belly. Neither Jim nor I asked any questions of the doctor. I tried to control my fear and hold back tears as my world tipped toward the edge of fragility. Maybe everything would be okay…if only I could have just heard something…something different from the ocean. *Oh my God. Why can't we hear the heartbeat?* I anguished.

A short time later, I felt the familiar warm gel on my belly again. The woman guiding the instrument was staring at a computer screen and had no expression on her face. I watched her, searching for the slightest indication of the diagnosis in her body language, but she remained stoic. I was growing more anxious and fearful by the minute. I heard the door open, and our doctor walked in. She stared at the screen for a few moments and looked at the expressionless woman gliding the instrument on my belly.

"I'm so sorry, Kelly. There is no heartbeat," she said, taking my hand and squeezing it. "Unfortunately, you've had a miscarriage. I'll meet you guys back upstairs whenever you're ready. Take your time. I'll try to answer whatever questions you might have."

I sat up slowly, beginning to grasp the devastating words. Jim drew me into his arms as tears poured from our eyes.

"We'll get through this," he whispered.

I couldn't speak. My mind could not let go of the present moment, of the loss I was drowning in. After we spoke again with the doctor and walked out of the examining room, my mind struggled with the fact that we had not been given a definitive physical cause for the loss, only possible causes. *Could this happen again?* I feared. *Why don't we have any answers?*

As we passed the reception area, my teary eyes caught those of my own mother's. Her usual happy demeanor and stylish dress made her the perfect office greeter at the desk job she worked in my obstetrician's office, but now her face was long, and her red eyes brimmed with tears. As soon as she saw us, she pushed her chair out and dashed over. She gathered me up in her arms and cried along with us. Jim wrapped both of his strong arms around us. Then the three of us walked out together.

"I'm so sorry, guys. It wasn't meant to be this time. But I'm sure next time, it will be just fine. This happens to so many women, Kel. I'm just so sorry," my mother offered.

I knew that my mom wanted to be a grandmother almost as badly as we wanted to be parents, and I hugged her again. Then Jim and I walked to our car, melted into the seats, and flooded the inside with tears.

As soon as I walked through the doorway of our new home, a feeling of guilt washed over my entire body. *What did I do wrong? How did I cause this? Could I have done anything differently to have allowed this babe to stay inside me and end up in my arms?* I lay on the couch in our living room and recalled that I had gotten poison ivy a few weeks earlier and could not stop scratching my belly. After searching the directions of an anti-itch cream for a pregnancy warning and finding none, I had lathered up. Now I wondered whether that could have been the cause, even though my doctor had said absolutely not. *Damn it. Why did this happen? What did I do?* I couldn't tell if my sadness stemmed from feelings of guilt, failure, extreme loss, or what. It just felt shitty and all my fault.

As my friends found out about the loss, I began receiving comforting cards and messages from those who had lived through the same experience. They felt compelled to reach out. They were empathetic and sympathetic and were the only people who truly made me feel like I wasn't alone. Their advice and consolation came from experience, and their connection to me made me realize that no one is ever truly alone—not in experience, not in feeling, not in success, not in failure, not ever. I felt a common thread weave itself among us.

Over the last few months, in Kathy's meditation workshops and various programs at the ashram, I had felt a connection to all of humanity across oceans and continents as we searched and longed for the answers to so many universal questions. Now I felt a more personal tie—one that went straight to my heart. I shared the same feelings of grief and loss as others, and somehow this bond made it easier for me to move forward.

Months went by until one day Jim said, "There are still a lot of extra rooms in this new house." He hesitated a moment, then added, "Do you think you want to start trying to fill those rooms again? Or, it's fine if you're not ready yet. It's totally fine."

I draped my arms over his shoulders and replied, "Only if I'm on top."

He laughed and drew me in for a deep kiss.

I'm ready, I thought. *I think I'm ready.* I felt a spark of excitement ignite within me, then fear. I had gotten on line again for the roller coaster, it seemed. I wanted to climb the heights and plunge into the depths, but my mind was terrified that I would get stuck, that I would feel the syrupy gel on my belly again and only hear the sound of the ocean. I wanted to finish the ride and hear the heartbeat; I wanted to hold someone new in my arms. I took a deep breath and led Jim into our bedroom.

After we made love, I lay in our bed and snuggled up to Jim's toasty body, thinking about the possibility of being pregnant again. *Please let this work out this time, God. Oh God, please*, I pleaded. I let thoughts of being a new mom enter my head and felt a desire well up within me to be a full-time, stay-at-home mom if a baby entered our future. Life was so precious, so delicate, a real miracle. I knew that I would want to be there to see it unfold. Any desire to climb a career ladder faded away. I closed my eyes and let the idea of a pursuit in motherhood take hold.

The next day, I walked into Jim's empty office in our new house to inspect the paint job we had recently finished. As I looked around the sky-blue walls, my eyes were drawn to the cerulean molding outlining the ceiling. Clearly, we weren't interior designers or professional painters, and it was obvious that we should have consulted a color chart. The hues blended as smoothly as my outfits in the '70s. The lack of furniture in the room made the incongruous colors stand out even more, and I was overcome by a new realization as I stared at the empty space. *Holy shit. How can I even think about becoming a full-time mom when we*

can't even afford furniture for Jim's office? The emptiness of the room stemmed from a lack of cash flow, not a fresh paint job.

This new office and the furnishings it needed were just the beginning of a list of expenses that Jim's single income wouldn't be able to cover—and that was without any children. I sat down on the floor and started crying. Jim walked into the room and bent down beside me, gently placing his hands on my shoulders.

"It's going to be okay," he whispered in my ear. "We'll try again. It'll be all right."

"I know. You're right. And I love you. I'm not just sad about the whole pregnancy thing anymore. I'm sad because…because I think I want to be a full-time mom in the future, and I know we can't afford it here if I do that—and we just painted your office." I tried to wipe the endless stream of tears rolling down my cheeks.

"Listen, this house is only perfect for us if we can live in it like we want. Sure, we could cut back on some things, eat more macaroni and cheese, if you want to be a full-time mom. But let's consider looking around again and maybe selling it. It's great, but I don't want us to be strapped when we have a child. I want you to be able to be home with her if you want."

"Or him," I interjected.

"Or him. And I just want us to be happy and live easily. Honestly, if we find something closer to the office, it'll allow me to be closer to work, too. This house seemed like the perfect place at the right price, but each day it seems like it takes me forever to get home. It won't hurt to look, and maybe we'll make a little money with all the improvements we made."

"Like the molding," I joked.

"Except for the molding," Jim laughed.

I hugged him, feeling my tears fade, and appreciating the fact that both of us were willing to make sacrifices for someone who wasn't even in my belly yet.

FINDING BALANCE

THE CERULEAN MOLDING didn't prevent another couple from walking into our home a few months later, smelling the hot cookies baking in the oven, and falling in love with the house.

"Well, we were lucky the house sold so quickly and that we're able to rent this one," I said, gleefully, to Jim, as I walked into the bathroom.

Through the door I heard Jim reply in his best Marlon Brando voice, "Yes, they definitely made us an offer we couldn't refuse."

Gazing around the cramped bathroom, I was reminded of how compact our living space had become in this new place. As I stood in front of the toilet, I could wash my hands and turn on the shower without moving a step. The white ceiling even seemed as if it was inches from my head.

"Hurry up in there," Jim said, anxiously.

I looked down at the aqua-colored tiles that made up the bathroom floor and drew in a deep breath. A few minutes later, I walked out of the bathroom, holding up a bright blue plus sign on a pregnancy test stick.

"Oh my God. We're going to be parents," Jim said, squeezing me in a bear hug and lifting me off the ground.

"I know. It's so exciting, but I think we have to be really

careful. I don't want to take any chances."

"Yes, fine. That's totally fine," he agreed, gingerly putting my feet on the ground.

Over the next few days, an amazing feeling of wonder began to settle inside me, and I recalled one of the vignettes I had previously read in Swami Muktananda's book. *From this tiny seed, an entire banyan tree grows.* Now there was new life inside me, and an entire human being was beginning to grow from the seed that Jim and I planted. I tried to grasp the miracle of it all, tempering it with cautious realism as I considered its fragility.

I started eating for two immediately and watched the size of my waist expand with each mouthful of food. First, I felt the tightness of jeans and business slacks, the muffin top that hung over my waistband. Then there was the improbability of buttoning or zipping any pair of pants without the onset of maternity wear. As I wolfed down hearty oatmeal, juicy fruit, and every chip imaginable, there was only one thing I missed.

"A salami sandwich. I don't know how much longer I can go without a salami sandwich. I think this longing has got to be coming directly from my damn Italian genes—or the ones you put in me," I laughed.

"Yup. That's definitely true," Jim replied. "But you'll be holding our child in one hand and a giant Italian sub in the other before you know it."

"You're right. But if I'm craving it and our baby clearly wants it, it seems like I should have it now. I'm going to ask the doctor about it again tomorrow. I know she told me to eat healthy, but maybe she'll give me the green light since things have been going smoothly."

"Maybe. Call me after the appointment tomorrow. Sorry I can't make it, but I should be able to get off work for all the rest." He walked over to me and kissed the top of my head and my belly.

"Let's keep our fingers crossed and hope for subs for dinner."

The next morning, I heard the quiet rustle of crepe paper beneath me as my legs dangled off of the examining table in the chilly air of my doctor's office. I considered the first question I would pose to my obstetrician revolving around her ban on cold cuts. After my doctor walked in and we breezed through her initial set of introductory questions, she responded to the subject that had been on my mind since dinner the previous night.

"So, Kelly, to answer your first question, salami sandwiches are still off the menu. Try to feed that hunger with something healthier. Cold cuts aren't nutritious for anyone—no matter who craves them."

I nodded my head in understanding, hiding my disappointment.

"I also want to talk with you about your recent blood work. The blood test that checks for things like spina bifida and Down syndrome came back showing a high likelihood that your baby could have some serious health concerns. The test isn't one hundred percent accurate. It only tells the likelihood or probability of this being the case. I'd like you to consider having an amniocentesis to provide us with more conclusive results."

My heart raced, and I felt a tremendous knot in my throat. At first, I couldn't speak. Then I stammered, "Yes, okay. I don't know. I think so. I don't really know what an amniocentesis is. Are there any risks in doing it?"

My obstetrician went on to describe the procedure and any potential perils. All I could think about was a *ginormous* needle going into my belly. The goal, of course, was to obtain amniotic fluid, but my mind was spinning. I looked around the bland yellow walls of the doctor's office searching for an answer. *Oh my God. What should I do?* I anguished.

By the time I walked out of the office, I felt more comfortable going ahead with the procedure, but I wanted to discuss it with Jim. I opened my car door and melted into the smooth leather seat.

Tears filled my eyes. I felt so lucky to be pregnant again and so scared that this perfect being inside me could be facing some difficulty. I rifled through my pocketbook, finally finding my cell phone.

"Hey, Kel," Jim said over the phone.

"Jim, it's happening again. There may be a problem with the baby. Some blood test came back weird, and the doctor wants me to consider having an amniocentesis."

"What?" Jim faltered.

"I don't know. Can you meet me at home?"

"Jesus. Of course, I'm on the way. Just don't think about anything till you get home, and we talk about this. I'm sure it will be okay."

"Oh God, I hope so."

I saw Jim's truck in the driveway as I pulled in. As soon as I turned the car off, he opened the door for me.

"I love you, and we'll get through this," he said, bringing his arms around me.

"I don't know what we should do," I cried.

"Okay, I don't know either. Tell me what the doctor said again. We'll figure this out together."

After we walked inside, I shared what the doctor had told me. Jim thought for a moment.

"I know the procedure sounds somewhat difficult, but I think you may need to do it," he said, solemnly. "What do you think?"

"I think so, too. But let me look online and see if there's anything else we should know."

Moments later, I sat down in front of a cold, emotionless computer and hoped that I would be led to factual information shrouded in soft clouds of delivery. I felt so raw and open, so sensitive to both the spoken and written word. Since there was potential risk in everything I did now, it seemed like each decision I made assumed an added heaviness, and my heart was beginning to feel the weight. As I looked online for more information about the procedure, I was overwhelmed with all of the data—positive and negative, founded and unfounded. Finally, I decided to stop my research and listen to my doctor, Jim, and my gut.

"I think I need to know. I don't think I can go for months not knowing if our baby has Down syndrome or some other difficulty, especially if there's a strong probability that she does. Maybe there's some stuff we should set up beforehand or some stuff we need to learn. I think I have to do it."

"I agree," Jim shared, sounding somewhat relieved. "I completely agree."

Weeks later, when the time came for the procedure, Jim was by my side. As we sat on well-worn chairs in the doctor's waiting room, I stared at the framed pictures of landscapes that hung on each wall. I wanted to jump into one of those pictures and be transported somewhere else, anywhere else. *Could that be why they had chosen the pictures in the first place—to remind you of somewhere else you'd like to be?* I wondered. I recalled that little family next to us on the beach. How I wanted a rainbow-colored umbrella and a tiny baby to play with in the sand. My eyes began to tear up.

"Kelly," a nurse said.

My thoughts immediately returned to the waiting room. I squeezed Jim's hand as we stood up and followed the nurse into a dimly lit, ice-cold room. My heart beat faster. The nurse handed a yellow examination gown to me, and moments after I changed into it, the doctor walked in.

"Hi, Kelly," the doctor said. "This procedure is going to go smoothly, so just lie down on the table and relax." Then she looked at the nurse and asked, "Can you bring in a chair?" The nurse obliged and rolled a chair in. As the doctor took it from her hands, she glided it toward Jim. The Italian sheen gone from his face, he looked the color of glue. "It's great that you're here for support, but I'd like you to sit down. I promise this will go smoothly, but we don't need anyone fainting." Jim nodded his head, and both of us laughed. "It wouldn't be the first time," she added.

I closed my eyes and imagined Jim did so as well. Both of us made it through the procedure without incident.

As the color was returning to Jim's skin, our doctor sauntered back into our room and said, "I'm happy to say, the results are normal—no genetic birth defects." Tidal waves of relief surged through my body. She went on to say, "Kelly, in all my years of experience, I've never seen a blood test that so strongly indicated the presence of some abnormality and an amniocentesis that ended in normal results. I'm so happy it worked out this way."

"Oh my God. Thank you. I know we would've handled this had it turned out differently," I cried, turning toward Jim. "But I'm just so grateful that our baby is okay right now."

Jim didn't say anything. He just hugged me for what felt like days.

Life was getting bigger than we had ever imagined. Our focus was no longer on just the two of us as a couple anymore but was now on the being inside me. And naturally, the balance in our lives moved in his—or her—favor. Our baby's needs were the ones we tried to satisfy, and we were realizing the ambiguity in even knowing what those needs were.

We were also beginning to taste the lack of control that goes along with parenthood—that goes along with life. Our lives and the life of our baby weren't up to us anymore, and in truth, they never really had been.

FINDING BALANCE

10

"DO YOU THINK I'm as big as that girl who turned into the giant blueberry in *Willy Wonka & the Chocolate Factory?*" I asked, staring down my body with my feet nowhere in sight.

"Jesus," Jim laughed. "No. Definitely no. You're beautiful." A hundred years ago, Jim would have joked back with me, but he was smarter now that my body and emotions were on overload. "Only a few days left. The doctor said it could be anytime now."

I nodded my head in agreement. My eating habits had remained steady, and my cravings for salami had remained unwavering. With each passing day, I grew more grateful for elastic waistbands. Days later, I heard the words and sounds I had been longing for.

"Oh my God," Jim uttered. "She's beautiful." He bent down and kissed my sweaty forehead. A moment later, the doctor placed our daughter in my arms for the first time.

"Oh my God, Jim. She is," I replied through teary eyes. "She's absolutely perfect."

Our newborn's skin had a magenta hue, and her eyes were still closed. She moved calmly and felt completely at ease in my embrace. I was in awe of her, never having seen anything more beautiful. My eyes remained fixed on her as I watched her breathe, listened to her cry, and held her like no one else ever. I knew that nothing could ever compare to this moment. We had created new life, and I was finally holding her in my arms. Inside, I felt a kind of love like never before…deeper, richer, completely innocent, and raw. A natural, motherly connection took hold, and instinctively, the entire center of my existence pulled away from my own drives and needs and attached to the center of this tiny being. Life no longer revolved around me. Everything I felt or did now was intertwined with her.

"Kelly?" a woman questioned from the doorway of my hospital room.

"Yes," I replied, turning toward the voice.

A stocky, middle-aged woman with chestnut-colored hair began walking toward me. Her long, sapphire skirt swayed along with the lanyard hanging around her neck.

"I have a little stack of paperwork for you to fill out before you head home with your new baby."

"Okay," I said, taking the stack from her arms. "Little" was clearly an understatement.

"I'll come back and pick it up before you leave."

"Thank you. You know I'm leaving today, right?"

"Yes," she laughed. "I'll be back soon, and it really won't take that long."

Jim was tenderly holding our newest love, Kailee Faithe, and I watched him as he stared affectionately at our precious bundle. His strong, muscular appearance was tempered by the delicate package he cradled in his arms.

I drew in a deep breath and sat down on the rubbery couch next to my hospital bed and began filling out the papers. The questions were simple and straight forward: name, address, phone number—until I came to a line on a form that requested the "mother's name." Automatically I started to write *my* mother's name as I had done for over thirty years before. Then it hit me.

"Oh my God, Jim. *I'm* the mother."

"Uhhhhh…yeah," he replied, seemingly surprised by my obvious statement.

I'm the mother, I realized. *I am the mother.* I smiled and felt a pang of excitement run through me as I crossed out my mother's name, and I began to write in my own.

Jim turned to look back down at our daughter, and I watched him gently tighten his hold as she began to squirm beneath the snug blanket wrapped around her. After a few moments, he walked her over to me.

"I think she's hungry," he said. "She keeps nuzzling her head into my chest."

I took Kailee from his arms and held her close. Within moments, I felt her latch onto my breast. I was in awe that my body could support her while she was both inside and outside of me, and I felt completely devoted to her.

"I wonder if salami will still be off the menu," I said, smiling.

"Maybe. But she's got Italian genes in her, so I think it'll be okay. I guess we'll find out soon enough. I just hope she likes it secondhand."

A few hours later, we began driving Kailee home for the first time. As we pulled onto our street, everything looked the same: cars parked in driveways and on the street, newspapers stuffed in holders, garbage cans set up by the curb for pickup—until we drove in front of our house. Pink balloons floated from our mailbox, our front porch, even from our red metal grill. *It's a Girl!* signs were posted on our doors and in our yard. Our friends and family had begun welcoming Kailee home before we had arrived, and we couldn't wait to get her inside.

Within days of her arrival, her presence was felt in every room of the house. Disposable diapers, handmade blankets, and onesies littered every corner, and her expressive voice became as pervasive as the air we breathed.

I heard the mild cry growing louder over the baby monitor. *Is this the "change me" cry or the "feed me" cry?* I wondered, lying next to Jim on the couch.

As if he could read my mind, Jim nudged me and said, "I think it's the 'feed me' cry."

"No," I whispered. "I clearly think I heard her just say 'Dada, please change me, and I won't date till I'm thirty.'"

Jim smiled, seemingly snuggling deeper into the couch. "I wish," he replied. "I'd even readily get up for that one."

I slowly rose from the couch, recognizing that Jim was right. It's the "feed me" cry. I felt my breasts tingle as I headed toward our hungry baby.

Weeks later, I found my translation skills improving. Of course, during the wee hours of the morning, I still thought I heard Kailee say things like, "Dada, come get me, and I'll swear off tequila forever," while Jim thought he heard something completely different and more like, "I definitely need some boobs right now." But our mistranslations were getting far less frequent.

As I strolled around the house with Kailee snuggled into my chest one day, the phone rang.

"Hello," I said, in a low voice, trying not to disturb Kailee.

"Hi, Kelly. It's Carol. Sounds like you have a sleeping baby somewhere close?" my boss asked.

"Right in my arms."

"That's so sweet. I guess you're loving it. I just got your message and received your resignation."

"Yes," I replied, gently laying Kailee down. "I can't imagine doing anything else right now. It still feels weird not to be working with you guys, but this job is 24-7. Thanks for understanding my leaving."

"If you ever want to come back, you know I'd love to have you. And if you just want to take some more time off without pay before I formally accept your resignation, that's fine, too."

"Thanks, Carol. That means so much to me. But I'm sure. I want to be here. Get someone else in there to give you a hand and head over here when you need a break."

"Okay, I understand. I'll talk with you soon. Good luck in your new motherhood career. There's nothing like it." Since Carol was a mom herself, I knew that she meant every word.

As I hung up the phone, I realized that my desire to become a full-time mom was woven in me even before I gave birth to Kailee. It was there as I sat on the floor of our first house, staring at the cerulean molding that outlined the ceiling, wondering if I would ever be pregnant again. The seed may have even been planted before that, as I pondered spirituality, marveling at the mysteries of creation. I felt so lucky now.

I looked around the kitchen and spotted a pile of dirty dishes in the sink. Kailee wasn't even eating real food yet, and the sink was still full. I heard a faint murmur over the baby monitor. As I walked toward Kailee's room, I laughed realizing the dishes would wait again. I gently picked up Kailee and drew her to my chest, settling down onto the wooden rocking chair that sat in the corner of her room. I closed my eyes, feeling completely content, and began to rock back and forth slowly, quietly chanting the mantra *Om Namah Shivaya* to my precious bundle.

FINDING BALANCE

11

EXTRA DIAPERS, outfits, wipes, socks, toys…I rifled through the diaper bag like it was an unfamiliar pocketbook and scanned Kailee's pale blue room for anything else she might need on our first trip to the ashram together. Since this was one of our first outings, I hadn't gotten the packing down to a science yet. I looked up at the border of cartoon zoo animals outlining her room and reached for a stuffed duck on a rocking chair. Then I gently lifted the car seat with my sleeping baby in it and walked to the front door.

Within half an hour, I was walking onto the enclosed porch I had been on countless times before by myself, only this time I had my child with me. I removed my shoes and stepped through another door, breathing in the smoky incense and meeting the waiting eyes and open arms of close friends.

"She's so beautiful," a friend said, swooning over Kailee.

"Thank you. I'm so glad she slept the whole way here. She's just starting to open her eyes now."

I looked over at the golden statue of the Indian saint I had grown accustomed to seeing. I placed the car seat down on the carpeted floor and bowed to the statue in gratitude. Then I picked Kailee back up as my friends and I walked into another room where we sat down, relaxed, and shared hot chai and homemade cookies for a few hours. I relished the conversation that rolled from breast feeding to mantras, to vacations, to chanting, to tofu, to pizza, moving in every direction with an easy flow like a winding road in the Catskill Mountains.

When the sunlight began to fade, I tucked Kailee back into her car seat, embraced my friends, and headed for the door. After a short drive back home, I pulled into our driveway and noticed that Jim's truck was already there. As I opened the front door, I inhaled the aroma of fragrant Italian tomato sauce. Jim walked over to me, kissed my cheek, and took the car seat from my hands. Although Kailee had fallen back asleep on the way home, he could not resist the need to hold his newborn daughter. He unfastened the buckles and slowly slid his fingers under her back, drawing her to his chest.

"How was the ashram today?" he asked absentmindedly, staring at our sleeping baby.

"It was great, and the sauce smells delicious." As I walked into the kitchen, I eyed the empty white sink and was grateful that Jim had cleaned up. "Everyone just loved her."

"Of course they did. She's got some beautiful rock star draw about her."

"Yeah, like Madonna—only totally different," I laughed. Before Jim could picture any risqué outfit or sensual song lyric in his head, I continued, "While I was there, I asked if the ashram offers any kind of spiritual service for newborns, like a christening. They said that some people invite a Brahmin priest to their house to lead a short ceremony where their child is blessed. Since we don't go to church and have found our groove at the ashram, I think this might be a nice way to have Kailee blessed. What do you think?"

"I think it sounds good," Jim replied, nodding his head in agreement. "Honestly, if my grandmother was alive today, she'd sneak Kailee out to St. Joseph's Church, have her baptized, and then shower us with holy water—all while we were eating her meatballs."

"Jesus. You're so right. Except that she might start serving those meatballs to us in the back of the church. She'd find some way to get us back there, and God knows, we'd follow those meatballs anywhere."

"Damn right," Jim replied, bringing Kailee to one arm like a football and stirring the sauce with his other hand.

I walked to the stove, carefully lifted the pot, and placed the sauce on the table. Then I grabbed a crusty loaf of bread off of the counter, along with a large bowl of pasta. As I headed back toward the table, I stopped and stared at Jim for a moment. He had sat down at the table with Kailee still in his arms. His focus remained on her, as if hypnotized by what lay in the cradle of his arms. A sweet feeling of family, of togetherness, flowed through me.

Weeks later, and without the intervention of any living or dead grandmothers, we began inviting friends and family to the spiritual service we had planned for Kailee at our home. Although Jim and I had been to numerous ceremonies at the ashram, our family and friends had not. We knew that when we invited them to this service, we would have to give them a quick Ashram Ceremony 101 lesson.

"So, it's like a christening, but it's done at our house with a Brahmin priest. It's more on the Hindu path. I think the priest anoints Kailee with some milk or honey, similar to the whole baptismal deal with water in a church. And then we'll sing some songs, and Kailee will be blessed, and we'll eat and celebrate," I said into the phone.

"All right, if that's what you guys want. What can I bring?" my mom asked.

"Ummm, I don't know. What do you want to bring? You just can't bring any meatballs or veal cutlets—no meat at all. We have to do this the vegetarian way because we're having a Brahmin priest here and some friends from the ashram, too. This path is more vegetarian, and I think that the Brahmin priest officiating might be a bit horrified if we celebrated with dead cow meat."

"So you're going to be having a party—with no meat—with your friends? Okay, I'll do what you want, so just tell me what I can bring," my mom replied, somewhat dismayed.

"How about a dessert?"

"That's fine. I'll do that—a cheesecake and some cream puffs."

"Great. Thanks, Mom. Thanks for understanding. See you later."

As I hung up the phone, I felt grateful that my mom had accepted the fact that our spirituality had swung East. This was really the only time that she had been affected by it; the only casualties—her delicious meatballs and veal cutlets.

On the day of the ceremony, our family and friends partook in the celebration like they had done it a thousand times before. Everyone had gathered in our rectangular-shaped living room, which had the spaciousness of a small cannoli. Like the filling, bodies were stuffed into every possible space, packing furniture to the very edges. The priest, dressed in what looked like a white sheet gathered in strategic locations, took a seat in the center of the room surrounded by golden incense holders, white cloths, bowls of ghee and honey, and fresh fruit. We sat beside him; Jim holding Kailee in his arms. The priest chanted in Sanskrit and Hindi and spoke to us in broken English. He asked us to repeat certain mantras. Then he anointed Kailee with honey and other ingredients from his tradition and blessed her. Our friends looked on curiously while Donna shot the front door a regular glance—watching for any signs of the risen dead.

After the ceremony was over, a friend from the ashram handed out laminated song sheets. The words on them were as familiar to our guests as Egyptian hieroglyphics. As we began to sing, I looked over at my parents who had their eyes locked on the sheet, thoughtfully trying to pronounce the foreign words. Donna even attempted to join in the chorus. Once the song ended, the Brahmin priest began picking up the items he had brought with him, carefully rinsing them in a bowl of water, and drying them with a white cloth.

"Okay, guys," Jim whispered to our friends. "Now, we head outside for the second part of the service. It's no big deal—just a chicken sacrifice. It's not too horrifying if you don't scream." Donna's eyes widened as if to say, "No way in hell," until she saw the sides of his mouth curl into a smile. "Just joking," he laughed. "It's over. There's no chicken sacrifice. Hell, there aren't even any chicken cutlets here."

"Well, I was hoping for something on the wild side," one of our friends remarked. "But I guess I'll just have to settle for you being a dad. That's wild enough."

Jim and the crowd around him laughed as he made his way over to me, standing in the doorway of our kitchen. I smiled and rolled my eyes, trying to contain my laughter.

"Anything I can do?" he asked.

"Yes," I whispered. "Try not to mention chicken sacrifices to the priest, and please put my mom's cream puffs on the table."

I turned and picked up a platter of pastries from the counter and handed them to him. As he removed the plastic wrap, the room filled with the aroma of delicious baked goods.

"They smell great," he said, drawing in a deep breath.

I nodded my head and leaned toward him, whispering,

"I'm so glad that the ceremony went so smoothly, and we only had a little trouble repeating some of those mantras."

"A little? I think half the things I said sounded anything but how they were supposed to sound."

"Well, your intention was good, and that's what matters, but you better not say anything to Donna or she'll be on zombie patrol again." I looked into his eyes more seriously and added, "I'm so glad we're bringing this rich, spiritual faith to Kailee. We've given her a starting point, her spiritual foundation, even if her wings take her elsewhere as she grows."

"As long as her wings don't take her too far out of our reach, we'll be fine."

12

SUMMER WAS IN FULL BLOOM as I glanced over at the billowing purple hydrangeas growing next to our driveway. I handed a compact stroller up to Jim who slid it between a cooler and a rugged plastic wagon in the bed of his pickup truck. Excitement was beginning to take hold as we sandwiched the final items into the back of his truck for our first trip to the Jersey Shore with our new baby. As I grabbed hold of our rainbow-colored umbrella and passed it up to Jim, he looked at me and smiled. The dream of becoming that little family on the beach was almost a reality.

"I can't wait to get there," I exclaimed.

"Me too," Jim agreed, eyeing the mountain of belongings we had packed. "But, Jesus, we have a lot of stuff."

"I know. I'd rather have everything with us than have to go out and buy it. Who knows what we'll need?"

"I just hope nothing flies out as we sail down the Parkway."

"How about you take it easy on the way down, Mario?"

"Of course," Jim smiled. "I've got precious cargo with me."

A few short hours later, we walked down the wooden planks that led to the beach entrance. I held Kailee in my arms, along with a cloth diaper bag and beach towels. Jim lugged our heavy red-and-white cooler, now stocked with fresh fruit, sandwiches, and ice-cold water, and pulled a wagon filled with toys, chairs, blankets, a tent, a rainbow-colored umbrella, and more. Sweat was dripping from his head before his flip-flops even touched the sand. I looked back at him and noticed that he was wearing his favorite, now faded, blue and green swim trunks that were frayed above the knees. After all these years in countless waves, the sea had yet to snag them.

As my feet touched the hot sand, I smelled the familiar fragrance of salt water and coconut suntan lotion. Then I brought Kailee closer to my face and smelled her sweet head. The perfume of the beach had changed for me, and I was enamored with the new addition. I dropped our towels halfway down to the water, unsure whether Kailee would be more of a sand or water lover, and watched Jim set up our umbrella. I spread out our Mexican beach blanket and enticed Kailee to touch the warm sand for the first time. As soon as her tiny hands tapped the smooth surface, she drew them back.

"Jesus, I can't believe she just pulled away from the sand. I thought that a love for the beach would be in her genes," I said, brushing the sand from her fingers.

"Shocking," Jim laughed. "I guess we've got to give her some time. Then, if not, I'm going to ask for a refund."

"Good luck with that. I think we passed that deadline once we held her in our arms." I dug into the cooler and opened a glistening bottle of cold water. "Want one?"

"No thanks. I may need to dunk in the water in a minute. It's boiling out here."

"Okay. Let's take Kailee down to the shore. Maybe she's more of a water baby."

Jim scooped Kailee up, and I followed him as he carried her down to the water. He held her in front of his chest as he bent forward and gently dunked her feet into the waves. As the cool water caressed her soles, she giggled and drew her legs up. I leaned toward Jim and kissed him.

"Definitely water lover," he said, dunking Kailee's toes into the water again and holding her tenderly.

As I watched him, I felt like I had it all—love, happiness, family—all of life's delicacies. My plate was full; my hungering for a child satiated. I felt content.

A year later, Kailee was sitting up by herself on our beach blanket, grasping handfuls of sand and letting them go in the blowing breeze.

"Well, thank God she digs the sand now—literally," I said, as I wiped the white lines of suntan lotion deeper into Kailee's forehead. "Are you ready to bring this love down to the water with me? I can feel the sweat dripping down my back."

"Sure, let's go," Jim replied. He picked up a dark blue baseball cap and pulled it down onto his head. Then he popped a pink denim hat onto Kailee's head.

When we reached the surf, each of us held one of Kailee's hands and helped her jump into the waves that touched shore. As I looked down the beach, all I saw were rainbow-colored umbrellas, pint-sized beach hats, and tiny hands wrapped around pink and green buckets. My eyes were mesmerized by the children dashing back and forth between waves. Two small girls in matching ruffled bathing suits filled a bucket with shells. Next to them, a young boy sat in the golden sand as the tips of a wave tickled his feet and edged toward his trunks.

A moment later, Jim leaned toward me and kissed me. I felt something familiar arising within me, but it had nothing to do with the kiss. I looked back down the beach at the children, realizing the feeling was clearly there. Deep within me, a fire was rekindled, and I felt the desire for new life again.

Kailee began to squirm away from our hold as her feet touched the next wave. Jim scooped her up and motioned back to the beach blanket with the tilt of his head. As we walked back, I grabbed his hand. When we reached our rainbow-colored umbrella, I took Kailee from his arms, sat down in the shade, and nursed her to sleep. Then I gently placed her down and moved into the hot sun next to Jim.

"The beach seems more crowded today, doesn't it?" I asked, sinking into my chair.

"Yes, it seems to get more crowded each year, especially today. Lots of little guys playing together—have you noticed?"

Yes, I noticed, I thought, laughing inside.

"Yeah, lots of sweet kids and families. Sooooo...I was just thinking...Do you think you might be ready for a little brother or sister for Kailee?"

Jim removed his sunglasses and got out of his chair, kneeling in front of me in the sand. "Kel, I think we'd be the luckiest people alive to have another baby together. The bigger question is: are you ready?"

"Yes," I whispered. "I'm ready."

13

MONTHS LATER, I looked down at the aqua-colored tiles on the bathroom floor of our tiny rented home and smiled. I walked out of the bathroom, holding up a bright blue plus sign on a pregnancy test stick.

"So, you think we're going to have a boy this time or another girl?" I asked jubilantly.

"It doesn't matter to me. A healthy baby—that's all I want," Jim replied, with a hint of restrained enthusiasm in his voice.

Unfortunately, the thought of new life didn't last long. Soon I found myself at the doctor's office again, covered in clear jelly, yearning for the familiar sound of a baby's heartbeat. I had another miscarriage. Luckily, my grief didn't have time to take hold because Kailee redirected all of my attention toward her. She kept me moving forward, and that allowed me to open myself up again to the possibility of new additions.

Months later, I craved salami sandwiches and found my body expanding beyond the outer limits of every elastic waistband that I owned. Jim and I were expecting a baby again. This time I did not have any unforeseen complications, and the pregnancy resulted in the birth of our second daughter, Paige Alyssa.

"Jesus, she's beautiful," Jim said, looking into the eyes of our newborn.

"She's breathtaking. Can you believe it? We have two girls—sisters!"

Within hours of her sister's arrival, our almost three-year-old daughter toddled into my hospital room on the hands of my mother. Jim bolted over and swooped her up.

"Congratulations, big sister! Are you ready to meet your little sister?"

Kailee nodded her head, and he placed her down on the hospital bed beside me. Paige was cocooned in a thin hospital blanket and nuzzled into my chest.

"Hi, Kailee-love," I bubbled, drawing my arm around her. "Meet your sister, Paige."

Kailee smiled and placed her hand on the blanket swaddling her sister and giggled. Feelings of elation quickly replaced my feelings of exhaustion. I looked up at Jim and, without words, told him how lucky I felt. As his eyes met mine, they returned the same feeling.

Weeks after we had taken down the pink crepe paper and balloons that had welcomed Paige home, the girls and I settled into a new routine. It seemed easier the second time around since I had some experience in the job. Nursing a baby, changing a diaper, making a snack, and reading *Goodnight Moon* for the hundredth time came together like the familiar ingredients in an old family recipe.

I felt less exhausted but more exasperated with the limited space that our humble rented home offered. A purple dinosaur and a stuffed girl explorer had become extended members of our family and were always nearby, but the other toys that lacked a theme song or TV show of their own were piling up all over. Bouncy seats and musical toys were in every room, and plastic bins lined the walls where furniture did not. Along with graham cracker crumbs, blocks and dolls floated on every piece of furniture. Our tiled kitchen floor had disappeared and turned into a colorful landscape of red, yellow, and blue foam floor cushions linked everywhere, and the large puzzle-like pieces drew the kitchen walls together.

"Jim, I don't think we can cram one more toy in here without completely blocking any way to get in—or out."

"Yes, I hear you. It's getting tight in here." Jim walked to Kailee and Paige's shared bedroom and eyed the space.

A twin bed covered by a pale pink blanket lined one wall. A wicker basket overflowing with books rested against a wooden rocking chair in a corner, and an antique dresser and changing table filled the remaining space. Matchbox cars littered the floor.

"I'm glad Paige sleeps with us," he added. "Kailee probably doesn't even realize this cramped bedroom is actually her sister's, too."

"Here's another issue," I said, nodding my head in agreement. "As the girls get bigger, so do the size of their toys. I can't imagine a life-sized purple dinosaur in our home, but if there is one out there, my mother will find it. And we will have to house it."

"I know," Jim laughed. "We need to start looking for a new house or some property—or we'll have to start sleeping on the porch."

Jim walked away to check on Kailee and Paige as I leaned against the doorway to the girls' room, beginning to feel another type of limitation that comes with a growing family. My children shared more than just a bedroom now; they shared me as well. From downstairs, I heard Kailee yell, "Mom," and a moment later,

I heard Paige begin to cry. I began to feel the multiple arms of my family pull me in different directions.

A few months later, I held Paige in my arms as I bent down to tighten Kailee's shoelaces, wishing I had picked up the sneakers that fastened with Velcro. As I stood up and looked at the forest that Jim was meticulously clearing away, I knew that we were on our way toward a home scattered with less plastic bins. We had purchased some wooded property, and Jim had been working on it every day after work since we had signed on the dotted line. He headed over when he saw us.

"So, what's on tap for dinner tonight? Something delicious and quiet? Maybe with some wine and a movie?" he asked, reaching down and tickling Kailee's belly. "You know it will be another late night for me here."

"I know. And you're funny. I don't think we've gone to see a movie or been awake long enough to finish one since before Kailee was born. How about some burgers on the grill and some iced tea? Maybe we'll even get lucky. If the girls fall asleep early, we can catch some reruns of *Seinfeld*."

"Sounds like a plan. Only problem is, I may be falling asleep with the girls. It was a long day today, and it's not over yet." Jim brushed some dirt off of his sweat-stained T-shirt and took Paige from my arms.

"Agreed. But I may beat you to it. Paige didn't sleep well last night and has been restless all day. I haven't stopped either."

Jim nodded his head, almost too tired to hold the conversation. He kissed Paige's cheek, passed her back to me, and then bent down to kiss Kailee. I leaned in and kissed his sweaty face. Then I walked to the car, buckled the girls in, and headed back to our rented home alone.

FOR MONTHS, Jim labored from dawn until dusk at his excavating job for his family's business, and then he worked for hours on our new property building our new house. He must have been a Siberian Husky or a plow horse in a past life because he never stopped. His work day was endless. Finally, we reaped the benefits of all of his arduous efforts.

I gazed out the kitchen window of our new home and into the wooded back yard. Then I looked at the floor, still covered with puzzle-shaped foam pieces, but more expansive in this modern, open space with windows linking us to the outside. I heard Jim's truck pull into our driveway and listened for a moment at the baby monitor before walking outside to meet him. Jim stepped out of the truck and stomped his muddy work boots on the gravel. As he headed toward me, I noticed the dirt and sweat darkening his bright orange shirt.

"Tough day?" I asked.

"Just the usual." Jim followed me inside as I walked to the stove and stirred a pot of homemade minestrone soup. "Smells delicious. I'm going to quickly shoot through the shower and throw on some sweats before we eat."

"Okay," I replied, grabbing some bowls from the cabinet.

I placed them on the counter and adjusted my favorite, easy-to-breastfeed-in, loose, button-down shirt and gray sweat pants. Clearly, the days of dressing to impress were over and so were the days where we had anywhere dressy to go. My daily attire usually included elastic waistbands and shirts designed with a smattering of different baby stains.

A few minutes later, Jim walked back into the kitchen in a loose T-shirt emblazoned with a Dallas Cowboys logo and blue sweatpants.

"I think the girls will be waking up any moment," I said, detecting some stirring over the baby monitor. "Maybe we can grab a few bites first." I filled the bowls and brought them to the kitchen table.

As I examined Jim's comfortable clothing and looked down at my own, our outfits began to reflect something more than relaxation and physical exhaustion. They also expressed a lack of romantic effort and physical intimacy. Sexy bras and thongs were alive B.C. (Before Children), but they hadn't made it into this next era. The baby monitors in every room floated our children into every discussion, every activity, every moment—including the moments when we needed to be alone together. And even in these quiet, infrequent moments without their presence, we chose to eat rather than wrap ourselves in one another's arms.

Then something else dawned on me—Jim hadn't even kissed me when he arrived home. And I hadn't kissed him. Our sense of togetherness as a couple seemed to be getting lost within the larger context of a family. It seemed as if we were only a father and mother now, no longer a husband and wife. Inside, sadness gripped my heart. I stared at my bowl of soup, stirring it absent-mindedly. My appetite was fading and so was something else.

As months went by, neither one of us stole an unsolicited kiss from the other or left a sexy sticky-note on a door, even though our children couldn't read. Our focus remained elsewhere. As I walked by Jim's desk one afternoon, I saw him checking out the swimsuit edition of a sports magazine with the eyes of Wile E. Coyote. He hadn't seen me watching him, so I walked away unnoticed. Then I stopped and thought, *I can ignore those salivating eyes or I can accept the fact that I have made no effort in the romance end of our lives and make a move.*

I walked into the room where Jim was reading and began to kiss his neck slowly while I allowed my hands to rediscover his body. Yet even as we became more intimate, I felt my mind drift to our girls. *Could Kailee walk in on us? Damn it. I should have locked the door.* Then I caught myself. *Jesus, I can't even let go of the kids now. What the hell am I doing thinking about them NOW?* I wasn't one hundred percent there, in Jim's embrace, in a moment that should have just been about us. *Check the light on the baby monitor. It's on. Thank God. We would hear them for sure. But will Paige wake up and cry for her favorite stuffed bunny? Damn it, mind. Let it go.*

After we made love and dressed quickly, I walked into the kitchen and started making dinner. Our first time back in one another's arms had been sparked by Jim's hungry eyes gazing at a magazine and my recognition of my own previous lack of interest. My heart grew heavy as I realized my marriage no longer held the same pre-children, perpetual bliss that it had years before. I opened the refrigerator door and watched all of the items inside grow hazy as my eyes filled with tears.

I spent the next few years floating and spinning in a whirlpool of motherhood and marital loneliness. I cooked, cleaned, and cared for our family in our new home while Jim filled his days with a busy work schedule, nurturing his children when he came home. We didn't make any intentional strides to come together as a couple. It seemed as if we had begun swimming in different waters, almost living separate lives, only coming together at the dinner table and then to opposite sides of a king-sized bed. Our marriage had become a steady lull of apathy, and I found myself turning away. As I held on to loving moments with my children, I set myself adrift from our marriage.

Then one day, when the girls were old enough to be in preschool and kindergarten, I found myself in the bathroom at Target where the pieces of my drowning marriage floated to the surface.

"Mommy, I really have to pee. Hurry with the toilet paper," Kailee cried.

I hastily grabbed streams of toilet tissue from the silver holder and covered every inch of the toilet seat, but after I stepped away and Kailee approached, she stopped.

"Mommy, there's a spider. Get it!"

I looked down again and eyed a spindly bug climbing on the inside rim of the bowl. I tried to capture it but wasn't able to, so I nudged it into the water instead. "Go ahead, Kailee, just pee. The spider is gone. It will be flushed away after you go."

"No way, it's still there. You go first."

I quickly whipped down my pants and followed her direction. Then I stood again to zip up. Paige, who had been oblivious to Charlotte and her web until this moment, peered into the bowl.

With the sound of terror in her voice, she shouted, "Mommy, did that spider just fall out of your vagina?"

"No, Paige. Jesus. No," I laughed, hoping no one could overhear us. "That spider was there before."

Then I flushed the critter away and repositioned some new toilet paper on the seat for Kailee who, thankfully, had a great deal of bladder control.

Paige's unusual question ultimately drew my attention to an area of my life that I had been ignoring. The passion in my marriage was dusty, filled with cobwebs, and basically nonexistent. *Yes, Paige, come to think of it, that spider could've fallen out of my vagina.* Jim and I had dropped into a marital, child-full rut, and we had not had the energy to find or make the time for each other. I realized that I couldn't ignore this part of my life anymore—for God's sake, spiders were making a home.

The next day I called a friend for advice.

"Donna, I don't know what I'm doing anymore. I see Jim after work every day. He's exhausted. I'm exhausted. We talk about the kids, have dinner, play with them, and then go to sleep. It's the same routine every day. I feel like we've lost something."

"Kel, it's bound to happen. Things change. People change. You have two little children now who need your attention and have become your priority. Someone once told me if you can make it through the toddler years, you'll be fine. I think most married couples break up when their kids are really young. I don't even know if that's true, but it really could be."

"Jesus, Donna. I don't know. Maybe. I have so much, you know—a house, the kids, a tired but loving husband. I know I have so much on the outside, but I'm not really happy on the inside anymore. And I feel like shit for even feeling this way. I don't know what's wrong with me. All things considered, I should be loving this fucking life, not complaining about it. And knowing that, I feel even worse." My eyes welled with tears.

"You need to talk to Jim. Have your mom watch the girls or I'll watch them. And tell him. Tell him how you feel. Otherwise, it's not going to get better. You need to do something about this before it gets worse. I love you, and I want you to be happy. It doesn't matter how much you have on the outside. It's how you feel on the inside. Go talk to him."

"I know. You're right."

I knew that I had to talk to the one person providing me with everything that I wanted. But how could I even broach the subject? Where would I begin? I didn't even understand how we had gotten so far away from one another—and I also began to wonder if he felt this way, too.

15

THAT NIGHT, after the girls fell asleep, I walked downstairs into the family room. Jim had fallen asleep on the couch with the television droning on softly. I stepped toward him and nudged his arm.

"Are you going up to bed?" he said, groggily, beginning to prop his weary body onto his elbows.

"No, Jim, we need to talk." I started to cry, feeling the floodgates burst open.

"What's the matter? What's wrong?"

"I don't know. I'm just not happy. We've gotten so far apart from one another. I feel like we've lost something."

We started talking about our lack of time together alone, our lack of desire to be alone, his life, my life. We talked, yelled, and cried. The deepest parts of ourselves let loose all of the shit we had been carrying for years.

"Kelly, I work a minimum of a ten-hour day," he shouted. "You're able to stay home and take care of our girls. What more do you want from me?"

"I know," I snapped. "I fucking know. But I need more. I need passion. I need you to appreciate me as your wife—not just as the mother of your kids."

"How about you appreciate me as your husband—not just as the father of your kids? We're both exhausted, and at least I make the effort."

"What effort?" I questioned.

"I walk up behind you. I pull you close—and you ignore me."

"I don't ignore you. We just have two kids, and they're usually a couple of steps away. And it's not just about the physical part. It's more than that," I cried.

But deep down, I knew that on some level he was right. I had dismissed his suggestive moves—the extended hello kiss, that purposeful bump when I bent over to pick up some toys, his exploring hands on my hips. Maybe I had offered him a whimsical smile back, but that was it—no welcome mat. My attention always seemed to veer off, away from him, and head toward our children or house. Although the distance between us stemmed from more than a lack of physical intimacy, I hadn't even left a door open for that. Why couldn't I admit even that to him now?

"Kelly, I know it's more than just the physical shit. I know that. Our world completely changed after we had kids. We are never alone. Never. Why don't we go away for the weekend by ourselves? No kids. Just us. Let's spend some time with each other for a change."

"Okay...," I considered, nodding my head slowly. "Let's go away...that's a start."

I looked down at our brown couch. *Would he go back to sleep there tonight?* I wondered, as I realized that neither of us made an attempt to hug the other. Maybe this weekend would draw us closer together, and we would hug then...we would sleep together then. I tried to let go of the doubts floating in my head, but they cropped up quickly like weeds in our garden.

Before we stepped into the car to head out on our private weekend getaway, Jim handed a cd to me.

"Listen to the third song. It's all about the perfect mother. That's who you are to our girls. They're so lucky to have you, and I'm so grateful for all that you do for them."

"Thank you," I mustered, looking at the cd and then back at him. "That was so thoughtful of you."

And inside, a piece of me died. He didn't understand. I didn't need any acknowledgment on the mothering end of things. In fact, I almost felt as if that role had flowed into our relationship, and I had begun mothering him with all of my cooking and cleaning. In my heart, I wanted him to look at me and see the one leaving suggestive sticky-notes on a door again—but I knew that I hadn't done that in years. I longed for him to see me as he did when we were in the prime of our youth, twenty-somethings, completely enamored with each other.

I walked to the car and placed the cd and my bags on the back seat alongside scattered Cheerios, remnants from the girls' last outing. It was the perfect place for the cd—the back seat. That's where I had placed just about everything with him lately—our feelings, our time alone, and now his present. As I considered his offering more sincerely, I began to wonder whether the gift he had given to me might actually be the kind of recognition he wanted from me. Maybe he felt unappreciated on the parenting end of things and thought that I felt the same. This wasn't what I needed, and I hadn't even been sensitive enough to consider what he needed. I felt the abyss between us grow. *Maybe we really don't know each other like we thought we did, like we used to. Shit. What happened to us? How had we grown so far apart?*

As we started driving to our getaway, Jim took my hand in his. I looked over at him, and for a brief moment, we didn't say anything. His hand felt the same as it always had. His grip was strong, and I felt safe. Without words, I wanted him to know how

I felt. I wanted him to understand that I wanted to be more to him than a mother, maybe even more than a wife. I wanted to be his lover, his confident, his best friend again.

The weekend away didn't move us closer together, except for the physical moments we shared in bed—and even in those unions, there was an emotional distance. After we returned home, I felt as if nothing between us had changed. I knew that both of us needed attention, appreciation, but we were coming at it from different perspectives. I began to wonder whether the gap between us could be bridged.

I opened the oven and eyed the bubbling melted cheese that was just starting to brown on the edges of the baked ziti I had made for dinner. Then I walked over to the kitchen cabinets, opened a drawer, and pulled out a thick phonebook. I sat down at the kitchen table and followed the scroll of my fingers up and down three columns of names of local marriage counselors. As I heard Jim's truck pull into the driveway, I looked toward the back door. A moment later, he walked inside.

"Mmmmm—smells like an Italian restaurant."

"Just your local one. Dinner should be ready soon."

Jim glimpsed the phonebook in front of me. "What are you looking up?"

"Well, honestly, I was starting to look up the names of marriage counselors. I don't know if I was hoping that our weekend away would be like some magical potion or something, but nothing has really changed for me, for us. I think we should consider talking to someone, someone professional."

After staring at me for a long moment, he replied, "Then make the call. I'll go."

16

THE NEXT WEEK, we walked into the dreary beige office of our marriage counselor, George. Framed pictures of degrees lined the walls, along with inspirational sayings. *After the rain comes the sun. Let your inner voice be heard. Yes you can!* George looked to be in his late fifties with graying hair and black-framed glasses. He held out his hand and greeted both of us in a strong New York accent.

"Hi. Nice to meetcha. Please sit down."

For the next hour, Jim and I took turns talking about our lack of desire to make time for one another, our lack of desire to be alone together, our lack of communication, our lack of seemingly everything. George offered advice and suggestions that we agreed we would try to thread into our busy lives. It seemed easier to agree to "date night" in the drab office of our therapist than on the floor of our family room with two boisterous children around. But often the best we could do after we returned home was to mimic George's voice.

"*Shaw, Jim, why don'cha tell Kelly about yuh day,*" I laughed, with a hint of Brooklyn in my voice.

"*Don't fuhgit to tell huh how you feel,*" Jim added.

Although we didn't readily leave the house for "date night," our terrible impressions of George made us laugh. And as we smiled, we slowly started to share more of our feelings with one another. I felt a glimmer of hope arise, thinking we might be on the right track. I still hadn't seen or put up any sexy sticky-notes, but I felt like they were at least in the realm of possibility…maybe.

Months went by and although we made small gains in sharing more of our daily lives with one another, the sensual sticky-notes never made it to the door. Somehow, we slipped back into our daily routines without joking, without making a concerted effort to share time, space, or feelings. Somehow, we grew tired of working hard on a relationship that seemed to come so easily years before. After Jim and I put the girls to bed one night, we walked out of their bedrooms and into the dim hallway lit only by a tiny nightlight.

I looked down at the shaggy rug below my feet and whispered, "Let's go downstairs for a minute. I think we should talk."

As Jim followed me down the wooden steps, I felt his strong stare on my back. We walked into the kitchen, and I turned to look into his tan, somber face.

"I know we're going to counseling, but I feel like our marriage has been on a downhill slide for months or years, or longer. I haven't seen any big change. Have you? I feel like counseling isn't really doing anything for us."

"I don't know what you're looking for. I don't even know what I'm looking for anymore. But I guess, no, there hasn't been any big change or anything," he replied, frustrated. "So, what are you saying? Do you want to stop going to counseling?"

I looked up at the white ceiling and drew in a deep breath. I had been going over all kinds of scenarios in my head since Jim and I had started therapy. Would we end up separated or divorced, or on some other track? I had grown disillusioned with the process, disappointed with the lack of progress we seemed to be making, and was ready to take a bold, new step.

"I'm saying maybe we should try something different—totally different. Something that would give us some real insight into what we really want. Maybe you should stay at your mom's house for a few nights or I'll go to my parents'. I have no idea if a few nights away will make a difference or not, but we're just spinning around without any direction. I feel like we need to try a new road." I felt my eyes fill with tears.

"I don't even know what to say. If this is what you want, I'll go to my mom's. I don't know what else to do. You're home with the girls most of the time, so you stay here with them." Jim's eyes grew red. He crossed his arms tightly, and I felt the space between us grow.

"I don't know if this is what I really want, Jim. I'm just at a loss. It's just the same—same routine, same lack of…I don't know…"

"Lack of what?" Jim interrupted.

"Lack of…interest…lack of passion…lack of being a couple," I replied, sounding defeated.

"I'll pack up some things. We keep fighting about the same things. I don't know what you want from me. I can't fucking believe this, but I'm going to my mom's. But I'm coming over every day to see our girls."

"Fine. Totally fine. Come over. I don't want to take you away from them. Look, I don't know what else to say or do. We're not really happy together. I feel like the kids are the only things binding us together, and that's not enough for me…for you…for us. Let's just see what happens with this move. I'm at a loss. I'm at a fucking loss, too."

Jim looked at me like never before. What was in his eyes? Hate? Disgust? Sheer frustration? I had to look away. Inside, I felt a mild feeling of relief. This move would either push us together or apart. Either way, it would help clarify things for both of us. A slight feeling of doubt crept up inside me. I tried to convince myself that we needed to do something drastic because it felt like we had been stuck in circles. Pangs of fear began to grab hold of me. What if I was happier without Jim? Or what if he was happier without me? *Holy shit. Where will this lead us?*

Jim took a few bags with him when he left for work the next morning and moved into his mom's house. Guilt washed over me as I realized that I was the real reason he left our house, the house that his hands had built.

That evening, when Jim stopped over to see our daughters, I invited him to stay for dinner. Everything seemed normal in front of the girls. They assumed he was going back to work when he left for his mom's house after supper, and they thought he came home again after they were in bed. They had no idea he was sleeping there, and we didn't tell them anything different. We kept that same evening routine in the following days and weeks. It was strange; I wasn't happier, and I knew that he was sadder.

My need for separation began to extend outside of my home. I started stepping away from the ashram. I thought that everything there should be perfect, and it no longer seemed that way to me. I focused on the imperfections, the human flaws, and felt my sense of spiritual fulfillment and community there disappearing. Deep within me, I wondered if the flaws I saw in the ashram were only a reflection of my own failings. I began to question the wisdom of the sages who believed there is perfection in the imperfect. I didn't see the perfection anywhere I turned. I didn't see it in the ashram, in my marriage, in anything.

Since I had turned away from my spiritual refuge, the place

that had offered me guidance and a moral high ground of sorts, it seemed easier for me to let go of the matrimonial promise I had made to Jim. "To love and to cherish till death do us part" no longer held the same bearing. It no longer felt rooted in my heart.

I was breaking away from the things in my life that had played such a huge role for so long—the ashram, my friends there, Jim, my marriage. It was as if the brakes were off and I was careening down the side of a mountain. I was trying to find happiness, contentment...to shift the balance in my life toward me—but was having Jim leave the house the answer? Was separating myself from the people and places that once offered me such love and solace the remedy?

FINDING BALANCE

III

THE GREAT BEYOND, AND THE DAWN OF THE EAST

FINDING BALANCE

17 THE HOUSE WAS QUIETER without Jim. Even though we had been on different pages, his presence had offered me the comfort of knowing that another adult, another parent, was in the home— willing to defend against an intruder, help with the dishes, or grasp the kids' math homework. Now I was alone. I looked around the empty kitchen devoid of the objects that came out of his pockets each night: coins, keys, receipts, notes. The counters were clear, except for the pink and purple cups that remained from Kailee and Paige's dinner.

After the girls fell asleep, I had time to contemplate what was going on all around me and inside me. I took a bottle of pinot grigio from the fridge and poured a glass of wine. As I walked thoughtfully toward the living room, I sipped the pale liquid slowly. Then I relaxed into a big, cushy chair.

For most of my life, I embraced the changes—career, marriage, motherhood. I spent years nurturing myself and my own drives and desires and then spent years nurturing the needs of my family. When the balance in my life shifted to my children, I willingly gave up my desires, or they seemingly vanished, so that it didn't even feel like I was giving up anything at all. I could not understand why I wasn't happy anymore—or where my course began to chart away from Jim. I took a sip of wine and held it in my mouth for a moment, pondering the questions plaguing me and savoring the dry taste.

It seemed that everything in my life changed once the idea of motherhood walked in. My marriage moved in a direction that I had not been fully aware of or wasn't willing to accept. My career aspirations became cloudy, maybe no longer even existent. And my individual desires became interwoven with my children's. The greatest treasures in my life had caused a monumental shift in the tectonic plates of my foundation.

Somehow in the aftermath of this gigantic internal earthquake, I wanted to return to a state of inner contentment. But how could I get there now? It had been over a month and Jim was still at his mom's house. I had no clear internal compass to follow; I was lost in a Bermuda Triangle of contemplation. I took another sip of wine and realized that I needed guidance and answers.

"No, I've never heard of her before. Ilene…Ilene what?" Donna asked into the phone.

"Ilene I-don't-know," I answered. "Hmmm…okay. I must have heard her name from someone else then. If I can find out how to contact this psychic, I think I'm going to see her. I heard that her predictions are spot on."

"Yeah, definitely go. You never know what she'll say, and it'll be fun, no matter what. I love hearing what a psychic has to say about the future."

"I know you do and so does your crazy ass sister. I hope I'm not becoming more like you guys or they'll have me committed soon."

After I hung up the phone with Donna, I called a couple of other friends, finally obtaining Ilene's phone number. As I dialed her number, I expected to leave a message on an eerie, supernatural-sounding answering machine. Instead, a woman answered the phone in a deep, raspy voice.

"Hello," the throaty voice said.

"Uh…hello. I'm calling to set up an appointment with Ilene."

"This is Ilene," the woman said. "Have you ever been here before?"

"No, but I know people who have gone to you, and they told me I should come."

While I set up my appointment with Ilene, I tried to imagine what she looked like. Her voice sounded so rough. I was expecting her to sound more mysterious, like an ancient oracle or a Gypsy from the Old West.

A couple of weeks later, I turned down Ilene's street and tried to recall her house number. Then I heard her raspy voice in my head: "You'll see the dark purple on part of my house. You can't miss it." I laughed to myself and shook my head—*dark purple*. All of the houses on this road looked like they belonged on Mike Brady's block; nothing stood out. Then my eyes caught the dark purple. Ilene was right—I couldn't miss it.

I walked up the concrete steps of her home and knocked on her front door. Ilene answered immediately. Unlike the Gypsies from the Old West, Ilene did not have a kerchief wrapped around her head nor did colorful clothes swing from her body. Ilene was a petite woman whose dark clothing hung from her bony frame. She looked to be at least seventy with short gray hair, reminding me of the little woman in *Beetlejuice* who smoked and saw dead people in her office in the afterlife. Moments later, Ilene brought a Virginia Slim to life and turned her head, listening for words from the departed. Clearly, the likeness wasn't much of a stretch.

Although she was kind enough to ask whether I minded if she smoked during my reading, it was clear that anyone who was worried about secondhand smoke would not have had a chance. The room was laden with the fumes of stale tobacco and whatever else was floating around in there from years and years of lighting up, doing readings, and channeling the dead.

Ilene and I pulled out tall cushioned chairs and sat down alongside an ornate dining table. As I gazed around the room, I had the feeling that I was in a grandmother's abode. Framed pictures and paintings of people and landscapes hung on the walls and leaned against antique furniture. A crystal bowl filled with hard candy was set on a side table among other glass knickknacks. Ilene's voice was the only thing out of character.

"The paintings in here are beautiful," I said, glancing at the artwork.

"Thank you. I did them myself."

I immediately wondered whether the people in the paintings were alive or someone Ilene saw from the dead. I was too scared of the answer, so I kept the question to myself. But then my heart skipped a beat as I worried—*Could she hear my question anyway?* Ilene picked up a deck of tarot cards from the corner of the table and placed it down between us.

"Shuffle the deck for as long as you like. Then place it back down on the table."

I nodded my head in understanding and picked up the deck. The cards felt smooth and looked tattered—from lots of readings, I surmised, or from the dead trying to get through. I chuckled as I thought of Donna's fear of chanting foreign words at the ashram but her affinity for psychics. Chances seemed higher that zombies would come more readily through this door than the ashram's— and the framed pictures might even be proof of that.

After I shuffled the cards, I set them back down on the table. Ilene put her cigarette into the groove of a glass ashtray, picked up the cards, and started my reading. As she spoke of the meaning of each card, she placed it onto one of three piles, moving from left to right. I watched her hands as I listened to her insight. While she was talking, I noticed that she had mistakenly placed one of the cards down in the wrong pile. As she reached for her cigarette, I interrupted.

"Excuse me. I don't know if it matters, but you just placed a card down in the wrong pile. I think you meant to put it here," I suggested, pointing to the pile she had skipped.

Ilene smiled. "No, the card is where it's supposed to be. If it's placed there, then that's where it's supposed to go."

She continued to talk about different people in my family while I pondered what she said and waited for her to talk about my marriage. *"If it's placed there, then that's where it's supposed to go."* Even though I thought the card should go somewhere else, it was actually already in place. Did I expect other things, different aspects of my own life like my marriage, to move when they were already in place? Had things around me moved in the direction they were "supposed to go"? Maybe there was more insight to this tarot card reading than merely the story Ilene was telling me.

Ilene's reading went on for over an hour, and she channeled my dead aunt at the end, although she used language that I don't think my aunt ever would have used. Unfortunately, the reading didn't give me the solace I craved. I wanted to know if Ilene saw me leaving Jim or him leaving me, an ending I had grown to accept since our time apart.

"If you have any other questions that I haven't covered in your reading, now's the time to ask," Ilene said, as my reading was coming to a close.

"Do you see Jim leaving me or me leaving him, on a more permanent basis, anytime soon?"

"No, I don't see either of you leaving each other. I see you together for a long time—till the end, as it stands now."

I tried to hide my disappointment. Then I went home and considered seeing a different psychic. Maybe *Beetlejuice* hadn't gotten it right. Maybe the wisps of smoke in the air had clouded her judgment. I called Donna and asked for the name of someone else she had seen.

A few weeks later, I jumped on Highway 17 and headed toward an old historic town, not too far from mine. I parked my car in front of a white, two-story house that had a sign in the window that read, "Hairway to Heaven." *This is it*, I thought. *Jesus—haircuts and tarot card readings*, a combination I hoped would be similar to Sonny and Cher or bananas and peanut butter—strange but nevertheless enjoyable.

I walked up the steps to the salon and began to smell cigarettes and incense. I opened the door, walked inside, and was transported to a place reminiscent of *The Addams Family*. A tall, furry animal that had been stuffed and mounted stood against a wall. Clear glass vessels holding potions, oils, or something from another world sat on bookshelves all around. Long crystals hung off necklaces and polished rocks were piled high inside wicker baskets. A woman walked toward me and extended her hand.

"Hi, Kelly. I'm Gina. It's so nice to meet you."

Gina looked like she had just stepped out of a time machine returning from the hip side of Salem during their witchy heyday. Her long, jet-black hair flowed over her shoulders reaching the middle of her back. Like Ilene, she wore clothes the color of midnight.

"Hi. I love your place. There's so much to look at."

"Thank you. I know. Sit down and we'll do your reading. Then you can take your time and look around."

Gina picked up a large feather and started gently brushing the outside of my body. She was cleaning me, I assumed, but I wasn't sure of what. Then she lit a piece of dried sage and danced it around my body and the area we would be sitting in moments later. She put the burning leaves into a ceramic dish and motioned for us to sit down on thinly cushioned chairs—thankfully, not the ones she used for haircuts. She uncovered a deck of tarot cards from inside a silky cloth and placed it on the glass table that sat between us.

"Please take the deck and shuffle the cards for as long as you like, and then place them back down on the table."

I picked up the deck and shuffled the cards. Her cards felt different than Ilene's—less tattered, smoother. Then I placed the deck back down on the table. Gina picked up the deck and turned three cards over and began to weave my life's story. Her technique was different from Ilene's, but I was astounded at how close their tales were.

"Do you mind if I smoke?" Gina asked.

"No, not at all," I replied, shaking my head.

I wanted this beautiful woman to be completely focused on my reading and not her next nicotine urge—even though I began to wonder how these psychics could foretell anyone's fate if they couldn't even see the deadly futures foretold on their packs of cigarettes. Then I waited for Gina to tell me about Jim's move away from our marriage—but she didn't. I waited to hear about my life starting over with my children—but I heard nothing in that direction.

"Jim is your soul mate," she said.

What? Not again. Were these psychics communicating with one another in some secret way? Or had the ribbons of smoke clouded both their centers of judgment? I had come to these insightful women to get the inside track on who would be the one to dissolve my marriage, hoping for an indication that my future held marital change and a brighter forecast, but neither gave any indication. All I had heard was "soul mate," "long time," "till the end."

I drove home confused and in disbelief of the fortunes I had been offered. Why wasn't I being given the outlook I envisioned? Those who were in touch with the outside reaches of the universe had not provided me with the comfort that I yearned for.

I began to question the separation. The extreme change I had prompted hadn't made me feel any happier or more content—and even the psychics could see that. The only difference I felt now was Jim's absence from our home and family and my guilt for being the impetus. Unfortunately, I still felt unsettled inside and was beginning to think that this huge shift had completely failed.

18

I HAD LOOKED to the beyond for answers and hadn't heard anything that confirmed the track I was on. I wasn't sure where else to turn or what else to do—and Donna only knew so many psychics.

"Girls, dinner is almost ready, and your dad will be here soon," I yelled into the back yard.

"Okay, Mom," Kailee replied, as she climbed after her sister on the metal jungle gym.

I opened the oven and looked at the browning roast chicken. The metal timer that it came with had already popped up. I reached for two sturdy potholders and brought the bird to the counter as I heard Jim's truck pull into the driveway.

Moments later, I heard joyous screeches from outside. I turned and gazed out the window and saw Jim swiftly pushing our daughters on the swings. They shrieked each time they pumped their legs forward and swung higher. I smiled and wondered— *What the hell am I doing?* A few moments later, Jim walked inside.

"Hi, Kel. Thanks for cooking. The chicken smells delicious."

"Hi there. It just came out of the oven. Hey, before you go back outside with the girls, I was just thinking…"

"Yes?"

"Well, I feel like we're in limbo—not really moving forward but not moving back either. What do you think?" I wasn't quite sure where I was going with this conversation.

"Kel, maybe we should go back to the counselor. We haven't been there since before I moved out. I don't know. Are you any happier? I miss you. I miss our girls."

"I don't know. I guess we could give it a shot. I'm not any happier. I don't know what else to do. Maybe now that we've been apart, things will look different."

"I'll call. I'll make the appointment for us. Let's talk without the girls around and see if there's something we can do before this separation becomes more permanent. I don't think we have anything to lose."

I nodded my head. "Okay. Make the appointment. I'll go," I agreed.

As I pulled my car into the familiar parking lot of our marriage counselor, I spotted Jim's white truck. He was standing beside it and began walking toward my car as I parked. Once I shut the engine off, he opened my door.

"Thanks," I said. I noticed he was still in his clothes from work and realized he probably had to leave directly from a job to make it to this appointment. "Was it hard to get away?"

"A little, but I told my guys I wouldn't be back after this meeting. I was thinking maybe the kids could stay with the babysitter a bit longer, and we could grab a bite to eat."

"Oh, okay. That might work. I'll make a call after we get inside."

As we walked into George's office and began talking with our counselor, it seemed as if both of us were beginning to look for new roads together. Hell, Jim had even planned a date for us afterward. When the session ended, Jim walked me to my car.

"I'll meet you at the restaurant in ten minutes," he said. Then he smiled—a smile I hadn't seen in a long time.

Our dinner was casual and so was the conversation. *"Don't make date night talk all about your children,"* I heard in my head as I recalled our counselor's suggestion. There was some talk of our daughters, but both of us made an effort to talk about topics other than them. It seemed easy to find mutual topics of interest from the menu to familiar friends, to old movies, to extended family, to the best Italian bread downtown. I had forgotten how easy he was to talk to, how much we had in common. I took a few bites of his burger, and surprisingly, I even found my eyes lingering on his a few times.

From that evening on, Jim and I started making an effort to spend more time alone together. We went on more dates with one another—reminiscent of high school, only completely different since we weren't living carefree lives anymore, and I had gotten rid of that fluorescent shirt and mesh overlay. We also started spending time with friends who had similarly aged children. While we savored luscious cabernets and gourmet meals with other adults, our kids noshed on finger foods and dinners with our friends' children in another room. We were laughing and having fun as a couple again, and our daughters were having a blast as well. I could almost start to see flickers of "long time" and "till the end" in our future.

One day, I found myself at the door, attaching sexy sticky-notes that read:

Leave your pants here.
Let me show you how much I still love you.

I had arranged for the kids to be at a friend's house during the time when Jim usually came over. As I heard his pickup truck pull into the driveway, my heart raced. I quickly scanned the house, wondering where I should wait. The bedroom seemed too predictable, so I decided to wait in the entranceway. I adjusted the new bra and panties I had bought and leaned against the spiral end of our banister, striking the sexiest pose I could think of. Jim walked inside with a smile on his face and headed straight over to me, drawing me close. He felt so strong and hard.

Then he looked deep into my eyes and said, "I'm still in love with you, Kelly. And I find you sexier than ever. I want this like never before. I want all of this."

I felt warm again. I pulled him closer and held him tightly. That was exactly what I needed to hear, and I felt the same way. I wanted all of this again, too—our marriage, our home together, everything. We made love slowly that evening, exploring areas that we knew by heart but had not shared in a long time.

The next day, the outlook foretold by the psychics began to turn toward reality. Jim moved back into our house, and we began working on our future together with greater vigor. We realized the importance of sticky-notes and making an effort to do things that once seemed effortless—because we had seen the consequences of what could happen if we didn't.

19

WE SPENT the next few years holding hands and romancing each other until we began to see each other as soul mates again. Our daughters continued to roll from one grade in elementary school to the next.

"So, what's up today?" Jim asked, handing a steaming cup of coffee to me as the first lemony rays of sunlight flowed into the kitchen.

"I don't know yet." I replied, taking the cup from his hands. "Carol left a message for me late last night and asked me to give her a buzz. Not sure what she wants."

"Carol, your old boss?"

"Yes. I'll give her a call after I drop the kids off at school. Maybe she wants to get together."

An hour later, I heard Carol's familiar voice.

"Kel," she shouted. "How are you? How are the girls? How's Jim?"

"Everybody's great. Everybody's really great. How are you guys? I feel like I haven't talked with you in so long."

"We're all busy, but really good. It's been a while since we've talked, but something came across my desk that I think you might be interested in. How would you like to do some freelance work for us? Help out with a conference we're putting on and maybe run a couple of workshops on youth development? Now you wouldn't only be a professional in the field but someone with some real-life mom experience to boot."

The girls are busy in school, I considered. Some freelance work...tying my motherhood into a job...going back to work...part-time...my own hours. It felt refreshing to be wanted by someone other than my family.

"I'm in," I said.

Through the phone line, I saw Carol adjust her scarf, nod her head, and smile. "I thought you would be. That's great. Hey, everyone in the office is heading out after work on Friday for some laughs and drinks if you care to join us. It's been a long week."

"Sounds great, but I have plans with the kids. I'll catch up with you guys next time."

I was interested, drawn to the idea of a night out with friends, but just going back to work in the near future was enough for now. Somewhere within me, I felt the scales of life beginning to tilt in my direction—and all without the frosty mugs.

The conference was a success and led to more work, ultimately turning into regular part-time hours. I enjoyed spending more time with adults and letting my creative juices flow outside of the kitchen and the family room. And I relished the fact that my marriage was on the upswing. As my work became steadier, Jim's world shifted in the opposite direction. He came home from work one night more drained than usual. His face was long and haggard as he dragged his heavy, muddy boots through the back door.

"It's settled," he said, sounding dejected. "I still can't believe this is happening, but Vince and I aren't going back to work tomorrow. We're definitely starting our own business."

"Holy shit, Jim," I stammered, drawing my arms around him. "I know we've been talking about this for a while now, but it's still unbelievable. Look, I know you'll figure this out with Vince, and we'll be just fine."

For months, Jim and his brother Vince had talked about some new developments taking place in their family's business. Things were moving in a different direction, and they had spent the last few months torn over their commitment to family and their need to start something new, something that felt right for them. They had been a part of their family's business since they had been playing with Tonka trucks and old enough to work, and their business was as familiar to them as their last name. These were life-changing decisions for all of our families.

As I looked at Jim, I noticed the tiny lines on the sides of his eyes. His expression was somber, and he looked beyond exhausted. I knew that's how he felt inside.

"I know it's hard, but we'll get through this change, and we really will be okay," I said, optimistically. "You have to follow your heart. We've been through so much. We'll get through this, too."

"I know," Jim replied. "I know," he repeated, not sounding convinced. I leaned toward him and wrapped my arms around him again.

After we cleaned up the waffles the girls had wanted for "brinner," I sat back in an oversized chair in our living room and closed my eyes. So much around us had changed. I had expected Jim's business, our marriage, practically everything around us to stay on the same path that it started out on. But life was unfolding in ways that I never would have predicted.

The words from Ilene's tarot card reading from years before began rising up in my mind. *If it's placed there, then that's where it's supposed to go.* Maybe life wasn't meant to go where I expected. Maybe there would never be a clear road map, a definitive course. Although I felt like I had already accepted so many of the twists and turns in my life, continuing to embrace new developments seemed easier said than done. Jim's sullen eyes were proof of that.

I started to feel a little unsettled inside. Was I still trying to hold on to paths that were changing or was this something else? Jim and I were standing on a stronger foundation. This uneasy feeling wasn't linked to my marriage, and I understood Jim's need to start his own business. I fully supported this decision. So, what was this restless feeling? Where was it coming from? Maybe, I began to wonder, I was starting to sense my own need for something more. But what more could I want? What was missing in my life?

20 WEEKS LATER, Jim hopped out of his truck with less sweat on his shirt and a happier demeanor. He walked over to me as I was kneeling down in the driveway, patting down the soil between the violet impatiens I had just planted in a black ceramic planter.

"Hi there," I said, cheerfully, coming to my feet. "How was your day? Did you get a chance to reach out to some of your old contacts from work?"

"Yes, and a lot of them sound really promising."

"Awesome," I replied, clapping my hands to release the lingering dirt.

Paige came from behind the house and ran to Jim, who scooped her up in his arms and kissed her cheeks. As I reached my arms around him and Paige, Kailee ran over to us and cinched her arms around our hips like a tight rubber band, yelling, "Family hug." After a quick tickle fest ended, we walked inside. I grabbed a couple of juice boxes and cold beers from the fridge, along with some crackers.

"Let's go sit on the back deck," I suggested, corralling everyone outside. I began to ask Jim more details about his day, and the phone rang. I walked back inside and picked it up, recognizing the voice immediately.

"Hi, Kelly. It's Kathy." Kathy had initially opened the door to meditation for me years before and had recently begun inviting me to different spiritual events with her, fully aware that I hadn't been attending the ashram programs for some time. "What are you doing next weekend?"

"I don't know, Kath. Why?"

"There's an amazing yogi coming to our area. I met him once before and loved him. I think you will, too. Do you want to come to one of his programs with me?"

As I considered Kathy's invitation, I began to wonder if this is what I longed for inside—the place where my spiritual footing could take hold again. Maybe I thirsted for a new spiritual cup of coffee like the one I had found at the ashram years before.

"Sure, Kath," I replied, intently. "That sounds great. Meditation and chanting on the menu, I assume?"

"Absolutely. I'm not sure if you've ever been to the ashram where the programs are being offered. It's about an hour away from the one you used to go to."

"Just email the address to me and I'll meet you there."

As the day of the event grew closer, Kathy called and told me that she had to reluctantly cancel her plans. Steadfast, I decided to continue to the new ashram alone.

I arrived at the unfamiliar ashram ahead of schedule and grew excited as I turned my car between two stone pillars that offered an unwavering welcome. I followed signposts that led me down a winding road to a long, one-story building replete with tall glass windows on all sides. Once inside, I continued to enjoy the lush ashram grounds around me. Mammoth oak trees and emerald bushes grew between numerous buildings and a pool. Gazing out the windows, I felt completely connected to the outside, to nature, to something beyond the room I was standing in.

I sat down on the floor among a couple hundred others. An elderly yogi was already seated on some larger pillows at the front of the room. He looked as if he was one hundred years old, thin with a long white beard. He wore soft linen clothes that twirled around his body like cotton candy, and the top of his head was crowned with a short white turban. His eyes were closed, and he was sitting up straight, but he didn't look rigid. His statuesque appearance looked effortless. Immediately, I felt an inner ease in his presence.

"As you meditate, empty your mind," he began in a soothing voice dusted with an Indian accent. "You don't need to focus on a mantra, or a feeling, or even your breath. Just close your eyes and sit quietly. Let nothingness envelop you."

I closed my eyes and breathed deeply. Then my brain went into overdrive. I wondered what the kids were doing, what Kathy was doing, how she would have loved this if she had come, how glad I was to be in this audience. *Oh my God. Why can't I stop thinking? I need to focus on something— my breath, a mantra—oh wait—nothingness…focus on nothingness…nothingness…just sit…is my nothingness black or white? Oh my God, mind! Stop thinking! I don't need anything—nothingness…nothingness…*

My mind fluttered between the word "nothingness," my children, Kathy, and what everyone was doing. I realized I was so out of practice. My mind wouldn't shut off. I tried to focus on my breath without words, then nothingness. But all of this concentration took a great deal of effort, and stillness of mind seemed elusive.

When the elderly yogi spoke again, he spoke about the inner guru within each of us. He also spoke of the benefits of meditation. None of his teachings were brand new to me, but they touched me nonetheless, resonating with something deeper. Then he invited everyone to partake in an informal ceremony in the front of the room. I rose from my seat, stood in line until I reached him, and repeated what everyone in front of me had done. I picked up a glass pitcher and poured water over his supple feet. Then I reached my hand into a ceramic bowl and grasped a handful of red rose petals and sprinkled them on top of his toes. Then I drew my hands together and bowed my head.

Knowing that the feet of a holy person are often considered sacred in Eastern traditions, I felt fortunate to be taking part in this offering and fortunate that his visit was so close to my home. I wanted to thank him, but the room was silent. Standing there, I wished that I could have gotten my hands on a bouquet of flowers—or on a nice loaf of Italian bread for him.

I arrived early the following day for the continuation of the retreat. I stood on the wooden deck of the glass-enclosed building, admiring the beautiful landscape lush with enormous trees, leafy bushes, and thick green grass.

From behind me, I heard a familiar voice say, "Wow, Kelly, it's so nice to see you."

I turned around and met the hazel eyes of an old friend whom I had known from time spent at Guruji's ashram years before.

"Jai, it's great to see you, too," I said, embracing my friend.

"I haven't seen you in so long. Did you move away or something?"

"No, no. I didn't move or anything. I just haven't been to Guruji's ashram in a while."

"Do you go somewhere else? Do you come to this ashram now?" he asked, leaning toward me. I could smell his cologne, and his shiny black hair reminded me of Jim.

"No, I haven't been going anywhere. I guess I just felt the need to step away. The only reason I'm here is because Kathy invited me to this retreat. I've been so caught up with my kids, husband, work, everything—just so much going on in life. I guess I've just been more focused on other things. You know what I mean?"

"Yes, I think so. But one thing I've found is that you can't let the business of life or a person—or even circumstances—get in the way of your search for fulfillment from God because nothing else can fill you like that. Nothing. That's what completes everything."

I looked at Jai and contemplated what he had said.

"Hmmm...yes...you may be right," I said, slowly nodding my head in agreement. "You really may be right."

For the rest of my time at the retreat, I turned Jai's words over and over again in my head. *Never stop your search for fulfillment from God...nothing else can fill you like your connection to God...that's what completes everything.* All of the things that filled me for some time still ended up leaving me wanting something more—my career, my marriage, even motherhood. I began wondering whether I had allowed my marital issues to consume me so intensely that they pulled me away from the one place I found my strongest connection to spirit. Or had I swam so deeply in the pool of motherhood that I began to ignore previous fruitful paths? Although I felt I had been continuing my spiritual search in many ways, I also knew that I hadn't been searching with the same passion as when I went to the ashram years before Kailee was even born. It also seemed that now my spiritual trek was dependent on invitations from Kathy and not necessarily from an inner calling.

Could Jai's words hold the key to happiness, to true contentment—contentment that never goes away? I wondered. Maybe I longed to connect with something greater, and I needed some thread of spirituality to weave itself back into my life. Maybe my sense of balance, my sense of contentment, did not stem as much from my outside world but from within.

I CONTINUED to contemplate Jai's words after I returned home. Within a few weeks, my phone rang with another invitation.

"Kel," Kathy exclaimed. "I'm heading to Jersey in a couple of weeks and thought you might like to join me. There's a wonderful Indian woman coming who's supposed to be able to impart her grace and blessings on to people through her gaze and touch. She's been referred to as a divine mother and teacher by thousands of people all over the world. What do you think? Would you like to meet her?"

"Sure Kathy," I answered, without hesitation. "Hopefully nothing will come up for either of us, and we'll be able to go together this time."

The night before we were supposed to leave, Kathy called me once more.

"You'll never believe this, but I have to bail on you again," she lamented.

"Oh no, maybe we're meant to meet over dinner and a few drinks."

"Yes, that could be. I'm really sorry. I wanted to go. Use my ticket. Find someone else to go with you so that you don't have to head to Jersey by yourself."

"Okay. We'll do something together another time. Thanks for the offer of your ticket. I'll see if someone else has a desire for intrigue—and maybe an appetite for some nice Italian food on the way home."

After I hung up the phone with Kathy, I invited Jen, a friend from work, who readily accepted.

On the day of the event, I dropped Kailee and Paige off at school and headed to Jen's house. As I pulled down her gravelly driveway, I grew excited at having a co-pilot with me in this unique experience with the divine.

"Good morning," I said, as Jen opened the car door. "I don't know what we're getting ourselves into today."

"I can't help you there. You're in the driver's seat—literally—so I'm definitely following your lead."

"Then, let's hope I don't get us too lost."

After a couple of hours on the Thruway, we walked into the spacious lobby of a luxurious hotel in New Jersey. The polished floor glistened from the modern silver lighting that hung high above it. I began walking toward a lanky man standing behind a mahogany desk when Jen tugged at my arm.

"Is that it?" Jen asked, pointing to a sign with our presenter's name on it.

"Great catch. That's it."

We followed the signs to a spacious conference room on the second floor. The walls of the hall were painted ivory and gold, and a huge crystal chandelier hung in the center. Hundreds of cushioned chairs surrounded three sides of a sturdy wooden stage set in front. The quiet room was sparsely filled, and as I scanned the audience, the diverse crowd seemed to range in age from their twenties to their eighties and to represent every nationality.

Jen and I walked to the front of the room and then down an empty row. Each chair that we passed had a piece of paper on it. After we sat down, we immediately started reading. According to the sheet, this renowned mystic saw two lines within each individual who came to her. The two lines would merge into one and show her where one was at on his or her spiritual journey and the obstacles that lie ahead. By touching one's head, she would remove the obstacles to one's spiritual development.

"Okay, Jen. Let's see what happens. I didn't see any Kool-Aid in the lobby, so that's a plus," I whispered.

"Definitely, but I really wonder how this whole thing is going to go down."

"Me too," I mumbled.

A moment later, a gray-haired gentleman in a tan suit stood up and walked onto the stage. He welcomed us as if we had been coming to these programs for years and reviewed the information sheet with us. Then he gave us directions on how we would get up from our row of chairs and meet the divine mother. Each row would be told when to stand and move toward the center aisle where we would form a line and wait our turn to walk onto the stage to meet her.

Minutes after the gentleman departed from the stage, a petite Indian woman glided into the room. She looked regal wrapped in a deep blue sari, her charcoal-colored hair pulled back in a bun. Dick Clark immediately came to mind as I tried to figure out her indistinguishable age. Silently, all of us stood up and then sat back down as she took her place on a chair on the stage.

Soon a young, professional-looking woman came to the end of our row of chairs and motioned for us to stand. Jen and I stood and walked to the center aisle. As we grew closer to the stage, we were asked to kneel on the carpeted floor. My heart started racing. I still wasn't sure what to expect. Except for the paper outlining the directions and general overview of the meeting, no additional guidance or insight was offered. No chanting erupted. No singing broke out. I was excited and anxious as I waited in the silence.

I tried to bob my head around the people in front of me to see what was happening, and before long, I found myself on the stage. I followed the same routine as the people ahead of me. I remained kneeling and bowed my head after I moved directly in front of this spiritual woman. She gently placed both of her hands on top of my head for maybe twenty seconds. Then she released my head, and I raised it in order to look into her eyes. When I did, I saw and felt only peace and love. Her eyes seemed so innocent and pure, like glistening pools from a fresh spring. I knew immediately why she was referred to as a divine mother. I saw the unconditional love in her enchanting eyes.

After I left the stage, I sat down on my chair, removed my shoes, brought my feet up, and crossed my legs. I closed my eyes. I didn't have to focus on my breath or a mantra, or even nothingness. My mind slipped into deep calm and quietness. I had the deepest meditation that I had ever experienced. No thoughts, nothing—just peace. It was amazing.

As I drove home, I began to realize the inherent benefits of spending time at these spiritual events, and I embraced the stillness within me.

A FOUNDATION had been laid inside me by the divine Indian woman whose eyes I swam in and by the friend who reminded me to never stop my search for fulfillment from God. My mind was fertile ground for Kathy's next invitation that led me back to the place where I had started my spiritual search years before.

"Kel, I just got an email from Guruji's ashram. I know you haven't had any inclination to return there, but they're offering a one-day retreat just for women with some interesting workshops on meditation, vegetarian cooking, ancient goddesses in Hindu philosophy, all sorts of stuff. I'm planning on going and thought you might want to join me."

For years, I had no desire to attend a program there and had sought spiritual fulfillment elsewhere. But now, I felt differently. I considered her offer.

"The workshops sound appealing, Kath—and I never really closed the door on Guruji's ashram. I just stepped away. Maybe this is the perfect opportunity to go back. Let me check with Jim and see what's going on that day, and I'll let you know."

"Wonderful," she replied.

Within minutes, I called Kathy back with my confirmation and with that of my friend Jen, who I invited as well.

On the morning of the retreat, Jen met me in the ashram's parking lot. I stepped out of my car and walked over to her as she finished putting on her makeup in her car mirror.

"Just a minute," she mouthed through the closed window.

I nodded my head and glanced around the property. The ashram had expanded and moved to a new location on tens of acres of wooded land with sprawling areas of rolling hills and grassy fields. It still lacked the belly dancers and cobras, but the expansive property invited more opportunity for international flavor. A moment later, Jen climbed out of her car.

"I'm glad you could come," I said. "I haven't been here in years. I'm sure so much has changed." I felt a twinge of nervousness run through me, as if I was surprising an old friend at his door.

Jen nodded her head, admiring the verdant land. "The place is gorgeous."

We followed signs that led us up a long dirt driveway. Beautiful flowers and manicured bushes outlined the landscape as well as the building we were walking toward. The structure was made of wood and semicircular on one end. It blended into the backdrop of trees like camouflage and looked like a natural outcrop—only with windows and doors.

Within minutes, we stepped onto a wooden porch, opened a heavy front door, and walked inside. I smelled the familiar ashy scent of incense immediately, and my eyes danced from one picture of a mystical being to another. Then my eyes met those of old friends. These were the people with whom Jim and I had shared so many momentous occasions—Kailee's birth, Paige's birth, the creation of our home. I didn't realize how much I missed them. I walked over and embraced each one of them, happy to be in their company again. Kathy brought her arms around me.

"So glad you're back," she whispered.

"Me too," I replied in a hushed tone, extending the hug a moment longer.

We walked into a larger room, and I smiled as I recognized the Indian saint embodied in the huge, golden statue at the far end. I bent down on the beige carpeted floor and bowed. I offered gratitude to this being, to the universe, to everything around me—for this moment, for my family, for my friends...for everything. I felt as if I was offering my annual Thanksgiving prayer of gratitude, one that always seems short, well-meant, and long overdue.

The first workshop of the retreat started shortly after we arrived. We explored the Hindu goddess of love, fertility, and devotion, Parvati, and two of her counterparts: Lakshmi, the goddess of wealth and prosperity, and Saraswati, the goddess of knowledge and learning. The questions posed and the discussion that followed allowed us to ponder those goddess-like qualities within ourselves. I reveled in the ripe discussion and then allowed myself to sit more quietly in the following workshop on meditation.

Once that workshop ended, I headed outside, wanting to see more of the beautiful land. As soon as I stepped onto the porch, I unexpectedly bumped into Guruji, who was sitting on an orange cushion atop a big, wooden chair. Because the retreat was focused on women and all of the workshops were being led by women, I did not expect to see him. Guruji looked the same as when I met him at Kathy's house years before—dressed in the familiar orange shirt and long matching wrap around his legs. Clearly, his time was spent on more important things than deciding what to wear each day.

"Oh, hi," I said, surprised to see him.

"Hi, Kelly, nice to see you."

My mind struggled with finding something else to say. What else could I say to the spiritual teacher I had left for years? *Hi, how have you been? How's the chanting going? Nice choice of incense today.*

I found myself saying the profound words, "You look great."

He smiled.

Oh my God. Did I really just say those words out loud? I cringed, wishing I could tap my heels together and vanish from Oz. Thankfully, Jen walked outside a moment later and stood next to me. I introduced her to Guruji, and then we walked down the steps and lost ourselves in the lush ashram grounds.

As I strolled around the property, I felt at ease. I had felt just as comfortable in the workshops among old friends who made me feel as if we were family reconnecting at a reunion. The familiar people and sacred space allowed me to sit and contemplate more than the conversations in the workshops. I began connecting the dots in the elusive picture in my mind…making some time for myself…embracing the stillness within…tasting different spiritual flavors and exploring deeper subjects that may leave me with a more lasting sense of contentment…The full picture began taking shape.

THE AMBIGUOUS, unsettled feeling within me was getting less invasive. It seemed as if the spiritual jaunts I had recently taken nourished something within me. I kept this notion in mind as summer rolled around, and Jim and I took our girls on our annual pilgrimage to the Jersey Shore.

"We made it down here in record time this morning," Jim boasted.

"I know. I can't believe how smooth the Parkway was. Since our place won't be ready for a couple of hours, do you want to browse around a couple of stores while we wait?"

"Sure."

Jim nabbed a rare, open parking spot on the street. As I stepped out of the car, I looked toward the sky and felt the sizzling rays of the sun caress my face.

"Love these sunny vacation days," I said.

"Me too—and it's just beginning. Let's head down this way. I think there's a bookstore right around here."

Jim took hold of our daughters' hands and started walking. We had only strolled a block when we eyed a storefront window lined with colorful beach pails, books, and sunglasses. After we stepped inside the shop, the girls headed toward a display of sunglasses.

I scanned a table under a sign that read "Bestsellers" and spotted a novel that had been recommended to me by numerous friends. It was about a woman who traveled to different countries and experienced spiritual fulfillment and love. I was drawn to it.

I picked it up and placed it on the counter next to the cash register, along with some markers and sunglasses that the girls wanted. Jim walked to the check out area, looked down at the book, and back up at me.

"So you really think you're going to finish a book while we're down here?"

"I don't know. Between the girls, the waves, snacks, bathroom breaks, sand castles, and whatever else, I have no idea—but I'm going to give it a try."

"Me too," he laughed, tossing a paperback about a famous baseball player on top of the pile.

Hours later, I drew in the fresh ocean air and smelled the delicious scent of tropical suntan lotion. I sat down on my beach chair under our rainbow-colored umbrella, opened the novel, and focused my attention on the words written on each page. I did not allow my mind or eyes to wander down to the people walking the beach or digging in the sand. My children didn't request any help building a sand castle or diving into a wave. I read page after page. I envied the author who had picked up and left home to travel to different countries, searching for contentment.

It was at that moment that I sent out a silent wish to the universe for a sign that could lead me toward my own inner fulfillment. I was starting to feel an internal need for a teacher, but I wasn't sure where to turn. Maybe this is what I truly longed for deep within. Maybe I wasn't in need of exploring different spiritual events and paths as much as I was in need of finding the right teacher. I began to think about the individuals whom I had recently spent time with. I wondered where I should turn. To the yogi whose feet I had watered with flower petals? To the divine mother? Back to Guruji? To someone else? I begged the universe for a sign to point me in the right direction.

Then I recalled all of the times in my life when I had sent out a silent message to the universe or to a dead relative and heard zilch back.

Nana, I miss you. I miss your unconditional love and my late-night sleepovers. Let me know that you're listening.

Nothing.

Nanny (Jim's Italian grandmother), we miss you—and your meatballs. Don't strike us down since we didn't have our kids baptized.

Nothing—Thank God. So maybe she was listening.

So-and-so's child is sick. Please bring him comfort.

No idea if I was heard.

But this time at the beach was different. I sent out a deep-seated need for a sign, and it happened. Within minutes, I read the mantra *Om Namah Shivaya* inside the book! It was the mantra I heard and fell in love with years' back at the meditation workshop led by Kathy. It was the sacred phrase I chanted for years afterward at Guruji's ashram and the one I sang to my children while lulling them to sleep as babies.

I could have read any one of the countless mantras in existence. To have come across this specific one while I was asking for wisdom from the universe was remarkable. I felt as if the universe actually heard my question, my wish for guidance, and answered me. I started to cry. Jim saw my tears and put his arms around me.

"Kel, what's going on? What's the matter?"

"Oh my God. You'll never believe this. I asked for a sign from the universe, and I got it. I really got it. Holy shit, Jim. I know what I need to do."

I spent the next twenty minutes reiterating my life over the last few months. Although he was aware of what I had been doing, until that moment, I had not understood how all of the pieces came together—how I had just realized my need for a teacher and how the mantra pointed to Guruji. By now, of course, Jim was used to my insanity, spiritual or otherwise. He hugged me, and I knew he understood.

"I'm glad you got your answer."

"Me too," I whispered, wiping the tears from my eyes.

A few moments later, Jim put his arm around me again and said, "It's good you found some direction. But you know, I could've told you where to go a long time ago."

"I'm sure you could have," I laughed. "But somehow, I know it's not anywhere I would have wanted to land. I know the coals down south will wait for me. How about I let you direct me to the cooler for a couple of cold ones and we'll leave the rest to Guruji and the ashram?"

"Sounds like a plan."

Jim raised his hand for a high-five, and I slapped it. Then I headed to the cooler and poured some cold drinks into red, plastic cups.

"Cheers," I said, handing the cup to Jim.

"Cheers," he said, tapping his cup to mine. "To letting the universe tell you where to go."

After our family returned home from the Jersey Shore, Jim and I talked about going back to the ashram. Jim had always been open to it and the yogic path that it offered. He was comfortable with the essence of the teachings, although his presence there was usually based on my lead, just as I followed his lead when it came to doing yard work.

"I know that all signs pointed to returning to Guruji's ashram for me at the beach, but what about you?" I asked. "Do you think you'd like to go back? Maybe with the girls?"

"I think I'd be willing to give it a shot," Jim replied. "And I think it will be good for the girls, too."

"I think it will be good for all of us," I agreed.

"I guess this means I'll be seeing the Big G-Man again also."

"Yup, and I think Guruji will be glad to see our family. And you'll enjoy hanging out with all of our old friends, too."

Jim nodded his head and smiled. "I guess the universe ended up telling us all where to go, Kel."

The following Sunday, we fastened Kailee and Paige into the car and drove to the ashram for a short program. As Jim stepped out of the car and onto the stone parking lot, he looked around in awe.

"Wow. They've really expanded."

"Yes. Let's walk over. I can't wait for you guys to see everyone."

Moments later, we pushed open the heavy wooden door of the main building where we were greeted by numerous friends. We reintroduced our children to people who they didn't remember but whom they were clearly remembered by. I felt a soothing warmth within me, like the toasty feeling you get sitting around a campfire with loved ones, as we were once again surrounded by the genuine affection of dear friends. I felt as if we had returned to our spiritual home.

A couple of months later, the leaves on the trees turned crimson and orange and began falling to the ground. By this time, our family had become regulars at the weekly ashram programs. Friendships were rekindled, and our girls were starting to make their own connections with other similarly aged children who went to the ashram with their families. Kathy and I were spending more time together at our spiritual sanctum and growing closer. After I dropped Kailee and Paige off at school one morning, I came home to an exciting email from my friend.

Dear Kelly,

You'll never believe this! I'm going back to India in December for a five-week yoga retreat. I'm going to spend the entire five weeks with Guruji at his ashram in India! I'm setting up all the logistics of everything now. I can't believe it! I'm so excited! Couldn't wait to tell you!

Love,
Kathy

I envisioned what a wonderful trip that would be for Kathy— what an awesome trip that would be for anyone. I emailed her back immediately.

Dear Kathy,

Wow! I can't believe it! That sounds so amazing! It'll be the perfect trip for you. I can't wait to hear more about it.

At some point in my life I know I'll get to India, too. And like you, I know that when it's meant to happen, it will happen. I'm so excited for you!

Love,
Kelly

I had barely hit the send button when my phone rang.
"Hell—."

"Kelly, I just had the most amazing thought," Kathy exclaimed before I could even finish my greeting. "Maybe it's meant to happen for you now, too. Maybe you should come to India with me. Jim and Vince probably have some flexibility in their schedules since they are in charge of their own business. Think about it. Maybe this is the perfect time for you to go to India."

I was speechless. I knew that Kathy had gone to India many years ago when her kids were young. She left her children in the care of her husband and family while she traveled, and everyone had been fine. I had always wondered how she was able to take a trip so far away without her children. For so long, I had trouble spending more than a few hours away from my own. But now, I was beginning to understand. This was more of a doable journey if the inclination was there—and I was starting to feel the inclination.

The ball started rolling. My internal tank began filling up. This ambiguous hole within me started to close. I had never created a bucket list, but I knew that one day I wanted to go to India, to the heart and birthplace of yoga. And I knew that I really wanted to go with my dear friend and spiritual mentor, Kathy.

"Wow, Kath. I don't know. Maybe. Jesus…maybe," I finally replied.

FINDING BALANCE

THOUGHTS OF INDIA started spinning through my mind like an endless merry-go-round and taking root in my heart. I kept the idea of this international trek to myself until it became too invasive—popping up almost daily as I folded laundry, ran errands, or made white rice. Days later, I decided to share the idea of the trip with Jim. I walked into our upstairs hallway and heard the sounds of a baseball game emanating from our bedroom.

"Jesus. What were you thinking, man?" Jim yelled at the television.

"Yanks losing?"

"They weren't—up until this last play." Jim's eyes were glued to the television, and his arms were firmly crossed.

"Gotcha." I walked toward him and sat on the corner of the bed, rubbing my hand on the moss-colored bedspread to smooth out the creases. The earthy shades and dark furniture gave a warm feel to our bedroom. I glanced at the television and waited for a commercial. Then I looked over at him and began, "Jim, this may sound crazy, but Kathy called me and told me that she's going to India in a few months and…well, I was thinking that I may want to go, too. I know what you're thinking—I'm crazy. And, yes, we both know that's true, but this may be something that I really need to do."

Jim looked at me, completely stunned. He leaned his head toward me, arms still folded, and responded, "Are you nuts? No, Kel, this doesn't sound like your usual crazy. This sounds like you're really nuts. Do you actually think that you'll be able to leave Kailee and Paige for any length of time without completely losing your mind? You've been with them almost every day since they were born. And they just started back to school."

I stared at him. *He's right*, a small piece of me thought. The girls had just started back to elementary school—the third and fifth grades—and I only worked part-time so that I could continue to be around for whatever they needed. And yet, I still felt drawn to the East.

"Yes, I know. I don't know what to say, but I think I want to consider going."

"Okay," he said, shaking his head as if in denial. "I can't imagine you ever going through with something like this, but if you need to consider it, consider it. How long would it be anyway?"

"About five weeks," I replied, with a hint of apprehension.

"Five weeks?" He shook his head again. "I'm sorry, but I can't imagine you doing this. I'll support you, if that's the decision you make, but I don't see it ever happening when you really consider leaving our girls."

"I'm just going to think about it. Maybe I won't be able to go through with it. But I need to give it some thought."

Until recently, I couldn't have imagined a day without my children near me, but something had changed. Something deeper within me was calling.

⁓

That weekend, Jim needed guidance on this matter and thought that I did too, so he invited two of our dearest and most honest friends over for dinner. We had been friends with Ellie and Mike for years. Jim had worked with Mike on numerous occasions, and I had drunk a few thousand glasses of wine with Ellie. We were usually on the same page and completely honest with one another when we weren't.

Mike came over, wearing his usual flannel shirt, jeans, and work boots. He had ebony hair and a black beard and could have been mistaken for Paul Bunyan's twin if he was only a few feet taller. Ellie had chestnut-colored hair and dressed more fashionably. She was sporting a fitted, lavender shirt and tight jeans. Round, silver earrings hugged her ears.

"Great to see you guys," Ellie said, as she walked inside and gave each of us a hug.

"And it smells delicious," Mike added. "No grilling tonight, Jim?"

"Not tonight," Jim responded, shaking Mike's hand firmly and wrapping his other arm around his friend.

"Come on in. Let's have a drink and a few snacks before dinner," I offered.

Kailee and Paige hugged our friends, then ran into the family room and continued playing at the child-sized plastic kitchen that was set up along one wall.

"We'll work on dinner, too," Kailee said, picking up a miniature frying pan with a plastic egg in it.

"Great. Thanks, girls. I can use all the help I can get," I quipped.

"Yes, she definitely can," Mike added, winking at the girls.

Jim reached into the refrigerator and grabbed two glistening bottles of ice-cold beer for Mike and himself. Then he poured a smooth pinot noir into wine glasses for Ellie and me. A couple of hours later, the aroma of lasagna still lingered in the air. The sink and dishwasher were full of dirty dishes, and the girls had galloped away from the dinner table to begin their own dessert preparations in their tiny kitchen. Jim looked at me and then turned to Ellie and Mike.

"Before the girls come back to the table, we need to get your opinion on something important."

Mike and Ellie looked puzzled. "What is it?" Mike asked.

My eyes met Jim's, and I leaned in toward our friends and shared, "Yes, well…I'm considering taking a little trip…to an ashram in India for a few weeks for a yoga retreat—without the girls or Jim, just me."

"By yourself? Oh my God, Kel," Mike gasped. "No way. No freakin' way. You couldn't do it—nor do I think you should."

"I don't think she'll be able to do it either," Jim agreed. "The girls have been attached to her hips since birth practically."

I looked at Ellie, pleadingly. She looked at our husbands, sipped her wine, and thoughtfully said, "I kind of agree with the guys. You know I hate to side with them, but I really do. I think you'll miss the girls way too much, and they'll miss you too much. I don't think it's a good idea right now. Maybe it's something you should consider doing in the future, when the kids are older."

I stared at Ellie and felt disappointment begin to arise within me. "Okay, I get what you're saying about the timing and everything, and I appreciate all of your opinions. I'll consider everything. I know it sounds crazy. I think I just need to mull it over some more." I raised my hands and shrugged my shoulders.

Mike raised his glass. "Kel, here's to you. Maybe not to India, but here's to you."

I smiled as each of us tapped glasses. *Here's to me*, I thought.

THE EARLY MORNING sun was just beginning to rise as I stared out the kitchen window, sipping hot coffee. Coral streams of sunlight reached through the trees that surrounded our backyard. Thoughts of India still ran through my head as I tried to weigh my desire to cross the Atlantic against my husband and dear friends' feelings of aversion voiced the night before. It seemed the lure of India was still rooted within me. I picked up the phone and called my friend Donna.

Before I could get all of the words out of my mouth, she interrupted me saying, "Oh my God, Kelly. You need to go. You need to do this. Jesus, this is the perfect time. I'll help with the kids, with whatever you need. This is the opportunity of a lifetime."

As Kathy saw it, so did Donna. Life had allowed things to be in place with my family and Jim's business so that I could seriously consider attempting the trip. I smiled as the previous night's opposition fell away, and the wheels in my mind slipped into higher gear.

A week later, I called my friend Maureen, who I affectionately called *Mo-z*, for a favor. Mo-z and I had become friends through groups we had joined for our children when they were babies, and we had remained close over the years. She was already aware of my prospective international journey and had offered her help with anything I needed—carpooling, babysitting, food shopping, hand holding, whatever.

"Mo-z, would you mind if I swung by and dropped the girls off at your house for about an hour or so? I think I need to go to the ashram and talk with Kim about India. She's helped tons of people make similar trips there, and I know she'll be straight with me. If she thinks that I won't be able to handle it, she'll definitely tell me. I think I need her opinion."

"Of course, your kids are always welcome here—with or without you—and I'm looking forward to hearing what Kim has to say, too."

Kim was a friend who had lived at the ashram for years and spent most of her life traveling the world on its behalf. She was the one person who knew me well and also knew what it took to stay at an ashram, away from family and friends and across oceans for weeks or longer. If she didn't think it was a wise idea right now, I knew I would have to seriously reconsider the trip.

An hour later, I turned down Mo-z's driveway, eyeing her children as they dashed over to meet us. My friend was in full-time mom mode, dressed in a tie-dyed T-shirt and shorts and holding a bag of pretzels and a handful of juice boxes. I jumped out of the car and gave her a quick hug. Then I squatted down and gave my girls a quick kiss goodbye before they ran off to play with their friends. Thankfully, they were as comfortable at her house as they were at our own, and I was able to slip away without explanation.

As I started driving to the ashram, nervousness and anxiety washed over me. I was drawn to India, but the reality was I had never been away from my children for longer than a few days.

So much of my decision hinged on what Kim would have to say.

After I pulled my car into the ashram's parking lot, I sat there for a moment and drew in a deep breath, the kind I might take just before jumping into the deep end. Then I began my walk up the familiar dirt driveway. When I reached the front porch, my eyes were drawn to the beautiful, fuchsia flowers hugging the outside rails. Their sweet perfume invited me to step closer and draw in a deep whiff. Before I had a chance to move toward the door, Kim opened it and greeted me with a broad smile. A moment later, the fragrance of sandalwood incense wafted outside.

Kim was a petite woman who usually wore her dusky hair pulled back in a bun, and this occasion was no different. The simple, pink dress that she wore hung below her knees and barely touched her curves. Her simple attire reflected her humble, easy-going presence. She grabbed my hand and ushered me into her office, and we sat down on two large, flowered pillows on the floor.

"Thanks so much for taking the time to meet with me," I began tentatively. "I've been considering joining Kathy and you guys on the yoga retreat in India. But honestly, Kim, I'm terrified of missing Kailee and Paige too much. I'm not sure if I can handle being that far away from them for so long."

"Absolutely go. You'll be fine."

"Really, Kim? Seriously? You think I'll be okay?" I embraced her answer but wanted further confirmation. "It's not like I'm going to be right around the corner or anything. I'm traveling halfway around the world. I just…I don't know…I just need to know that I won't be so consumed with them that I won't be able to handle it."

"Kelly, I've seen thousands of people come and go to India, and I know—I absolutely know—you'll be fine."

"Okay," I said, feeling my hesitation lift. "Okay, thank you. You know I totally trust you."

"I know you do. And I would never tell you that you'll be fine if I didn't believe it."

I leaned forward to hug her. "Then I need to get some basic travel information from you so that I can talk with Jim and see if I can make this happen." Within moments, our discussion moved on to passports and flight schedules.

When I stepped back into my car, I sank into the seat, feeling relieved and excited. I let the reality of the trip begin to take hold. *Holy shit. India! Kim thinks I can do this. I may actually go!*

I drove back to Mo-z's house, my head spinning with thoughts about India and all of the planning that this trip would entail. I zipped up her driveway, hopped out of my car, and darted to her back door.

"Thanks so much for watching the girls," I said, as I walked through the doorway into her spacious kitchen, eyeing a table scattered with construction paper, crayons, and glitter.

"No problem. It was easy. The kids have been playing the whole time. So what happened? What did Kim say? You think you're going?" Her eyes widened with excitement, as she brushed away some crayons and motioned for me to sit down.

"Yes, I think I'm going." Thrill ran through my body. "I just have to confirm with Jim, of course. Kim thinks that I'll be able to do it, and honestly, if she didn't think that I could, I would never attempt it. I still can't believe this, Mo-z, but I really think I'm going." Our children's voices floated into the room, and my excitement was immediately tempered by apprehension. "I dread telling the girls."

"Kel, I think it's amazing. You're a great role model for your daughters, and someday, they'll look back on this and realize how strong a woman you are."

"Jesus, I needed to hear that. That means the world to me. Thank you." My eyes filled with tears.

I needed to hear those words from my friend, a fellow mother who knew how I would long to hold my children when we were apart and who also understood how I longed to embark on this journey.

An hour later, Kailee, Paige, and I headed back home. When we pulled into the driveway, I spotted Jim's truck, and my heart raced as I realized I was moments away from hearing Jim's final thoughts on the trip.

"Daddy's home!" Paige exclaimed, as she eyed her father's pickup truck.

"Yes. Just do me a favor and put away all of the things you brought over to Mo-z's house before you start playing something else." I wanted an extra minute alone with Jim before the girls engulfed him in their activities.

After we walked inside, Jim yelled from upstairs, "Hi, guys."

"Hi, Jim," I shouted back, as the girls ran upstairs to greet their dad and begin putting their toys away.

I looked up the steps and drew a deep breath in as I took my first step toward him. *Here we go*, I thought. Jim was putting clean T-shirts into a drawer when I walked into our bedroom. I walked over to him and gave him a quick kiss.

"So I saw Kim today."

"Oh. You did? What did she say?"

"Well, she said that she thinks I'll be fine. She totally thinks I'll be fine in India. And honestly, I think I will be, too." I looked deep into his dark eyes and shared, "I think I need to do this. I feel like I really need to go to India."

Jim stared at me for a long moment. "Honestly, Kel, I don't

know how you're going to do it. But if it's something you feel this strongly about, we'll make it happen. And the kids will be fine."

I reached my arms around him. "Thank you, Jim. Oh my God. Thank you so much." Tears streamed down my face as I whispered, "You've given me the greatest gift in all our years together."

We held each other tightly, neither of us wanting to let go.

After Jim left for work the next morning, I walked upstairs and into Kailee's room. I gazed at her limber body relaxed in a sound sleep. I watched her breathe. Then I meandered into Paige's room and enjoyed the same sweet picture. As they slept, they had no idea about my plans. I considered telling them after they woke up, so they could begin settling into the idea.

I tiptoed downstairs and sat at the kitchen table with a steaming cup of coffee. *Maybe they'll be okay with this*, I thought. Perhaps they would be surprised at first, maybe a little hesitant, but then they would accept it like they do brussels sprouts with dinner. Within minutes, I heard the pitter-patter of bare feet scampering down the steps.

"Good morning, loves," I said.

"Good morning. I'm hungry. What's for breakfast?" Paige asked.

"How about some cereal, eggs, or cinnamon toast?"

"Okay. Let me look," Paige replied, opening the kitchen cabinet.

"I'll have some cinnamon toast, please," Kailee said.

"Me too," Paige instantly agreed.

Realizing how often Paige seemed to follow her big sister's lead, I hoped that Kailee would be on board with this trip. I glanced at Kailee, silently trying to persuade her with my thoughts. After the girls ate breakfast, they meandered to the family room, and I followed a few steps behind.

"Girls, can you come and sit down on the couch with me for a minute?"

"Sure. Do you want us to cook something for you in our kitchen first?" Kailee offered.

"Not yet, but maybe later."

I tapped my hands on the velvety, brown couch and allowed the girls to sandwich me between them. I felt like the center of an Oreo and hoped that they would swallow the upcoming news as easily as the cookie. I put my arms around them, closed my eyes, and squeezed them for a moment. *Please let them be okay with this*, I begged the universe.

"Girls, you know I love you both so much. And you know how much I enjoy going to the ashram and learning there, right?"

"Yeah," they said, almost in unison.

"Well, I think I need to go and learn more. But the thing is… I can only do that in India, where the ashram is offering a special program."

"What? Mom—NO," Kailee stammered.

Paige looked over at her sister and then at me and cried, "Mom, where would we go? Who's going to take care of us?"

"Your dad. Your dad will be here. And I'll only be gone a few weeks. And I'll set up all the plans so that you can see your friends and keep going to Brownies, yoga, and everything else. This will be a really special time for you to spend with your dad. And before you know it, I'll be back home. The time will fly by."

"Mom—NO. No, you can't go. NO," they shouted. Both of them started crying, and I fought to hold back my own tears.

"Mom, when is this happening?" Kailee asked.

"Well, I think I'd leave around New Year's Eve when the program starts and then be back in a quick, few weeks."

"You'll miss my birthday," Kailee cried. "How could you do that?"

I could barely speak. Missing her birthday was one of the major reasons that I had considered not going at all. I had agonized over this fact even before I shared the idea of the trip with Jim.

"Kailee, we'll celebrate your birthday before I leave for India and then again, after I come home. Your dad will be here to celebrate with you while I'm away. You will have a minimum of three parties with all the people who love you. And I'll be back before you know it."

I tightened my hold around her, but it didn't seem to comfort her. Unfortunately, Kailee was old enough to realize that parties are no replacement for people.

I began to regret sharing this news without Jim present. I had chosen to tell our daughters on my own, hoping to alleviate their fears without burdening him or allowing him to see any of their heartbreaking dissension. I thought that I could do it by myself, but now I realized I should have included him in this discussion. Maybe he would have shared things differently—in a way they could have understood or accepted more readily. I needed him and so did the girls, and I was just beginning to understand how much.

Although I felt my children's pain with every tear shed and dissenting word spoken, I still knew that I needed to take this voyage and give myself this time. Deep down, I held on to my determination, knowing that if I gave in to their feelings, I would have to let go of the string, release the kite, and watch the time I needed to give myself fly away. I needed to trust my gut and nurture something within me. I would have to do whatever I could to make it up to them. A pony, a car, and a unicorn were all on the table now.

The trip was scheduled to take place in less than three months. I had three months to ease my children's opposition, to break down the walls they were building with every thought of me boarding a plane to a place they had only recently heard of. I needed to show them that things would be fine while I was away, and everything would go on as usual. School would continue. Lunches would get made. Homework would get done. Friends would come over. We would all be safe and get through this in no time. And now I realized Jim's demonstrated support was paramount to my efforts and my children's acceptance. Like the sturdy beams he had built into our house, his strength and support needed to be integrated into these family discussions.

Within me, the longing for something, the unsettledness, the something stirring had calmed. I allowed my excitement for the trip to take hold within me, but I restrained it with the acknowledgment that I still had so much to do. I knew that this was the trip of a lifetime, and I also knew that I had numerous hurdles to overcome before I would even be able to take off.

FINDING BALANCE

A MONTH LATER, Halloween arrived with the typical fanfare: cobweb decorations on the front porch, candles illuminating jack-o'-lanterns on the steps, and lots and lots of candy. The autumn New York air held a crispness only paralleled by the first bite of a juicy McIntosh apple, and our children's costumes paid the price. By the end of the night, both of their outfits were partly hidden under an onyx sweat jacket and an ivory cable-knit sweater.

"I can't believe that lady gave out big candy bars," Paige exclaimed.

"I know. And that other lady gave out raisins," Kailee agreed, grimacing.

I looked toward the back seat and smiled. "You guys can have one more candy, and then we're having dinner at your grandparents' house and some birthday cake for your dad."

Giggling erupted from the back seat as I heard little hands digging feverishly through bags of candy. As we pulled into my parents' driveway, Jim looked over at me.

"You haven't said anything to your parents about your trip yet, right?"

"Right."

Moments later, Kailee and Paige scrambled up the front steps of my parents' house and knocked on their door. As the door opened, my dad's eyes lit up.

"What do we have here? A witch and a dead bride?"

"I'm a zombie's bride," Paige exclaimed, clearly out of the princess stage of dress-up.

"Aaaaahhhh. I should've known."

Kailee and Paige gave my dad a quick hug, then dashed behind him and gave one to my mom. My mom picked up a black wicker basket filled with chocolate bars and handed it to them, watching as they began passing out the remaining candy to other trick-or-treaters. Jim and I allowed a few clowns and vampires to pass before we moved onto the porch, meticulously avoiding the stringy cobwebs.

"Hi, Dad," I said, leaning in and giving him a quick peck. "Happy Halloween."

"Happy Halloween, guys. The kids look great."

My mom walked onto the porch, waving us inside. "I'm so glad you guys could come over. I'm already putting dinner on the table."

"Great. We're starving. Let me give you a hand," I offered.

Once inside, I was overcome by the rich smell of eggplant parmigiana and tomato sauce. Jim and my dad began chatting about football while my mom and I headed to the kitchen to finish putting dinner on the table. My excitement about the trip was beginning to take hold, and it blinded any rational sense of timing.

"Mom, I have some news."

"You're pregnant," she said with wide, open eyes.

"No, Mom. Jesus. No. It's something different—totally different. I have this great opportunity to go to India for a yoga retreat for five weeks in January and February. It looks amazing, and I think I'm going."

It was as if I said I was moving to the mountains of Afghanistan and never returning. All of my mom's Italian blood ran through her veins like fire, and I saw the memorable egg whites of her eyes that I only saw as a teenager right before I was grounded for life. I immediately felt sixteen years old all over again.

"Are you crazy? Do you know what's going on in the world today? What about Kailee and Paige? Have you even thought about them? Who's going to take care of them? Jesus, Kelly, you could be killed," she fumed.

"Mom, stop. I know the people who will be taking care of me. I'm going to be fine and so are the girls."

"Kelly, all you're thinking about is yourself—not your family or your kids. I can't believe you're even considering leaving your children and doing something like this," she yelled. "Your job is to care for and protect your children—not to leave them. How could you even entertain an idea like this?"

With each angry word said, she tried to make me see things as she saw them. Since she had never been out of the country, the thought of me leaving the security of home, for any reason, seemed senseless to her. In her eyes, I needed to remain steadfast next to my children—her grandchildren—period.

From the other room, my dad had heard the fury in my mom's voice. He had not heard about my plans yet, but he stepped in ready to douse the fire. He drew my mom into the living room, but I could hear her shouting at him. She walked back into the kitchen incensed.

"Mom, we're all going to be fine. We can talk about this later. I didn't know you would react like this, and I don't want the kids to hear you."

"You don't want the kids to hear?" she said, seemingly astounded, her voice growing louder again. "You mean the kids who you're leaving, to go to some far-off land, to do whatever you want? Those kids, you mean?"

"Yes, Mom—those kids," I said, trying to stifle my own frustration. "If you don't stop yelling, we're leaving. I mean it."

Most of the food had already been placed on the table when I dropped the bomb on my mom in the kitchen, but she had lost her appetite, as had I. She walked back into the living room and sat on her sapphire antique couch by herself, seething. She could not bear to look at me, let alone sit with me.

Jim, my dad, and our girls walked into the dining room and started eating an extremely fast dinner. I followed them into the room and glanced at all of the framed family photos hanging on the walls. Some were in black and white; others were in color, the older ones almost looking airbrushed. Family was the most important thing in my mother's life. She cherished it like nothing else and was averse to anything that had the slightest hint of risk. Growing up, my brother and I weren't even allowed to carve jack-o'-lanterns with knives. Instead, my mother had us decorate our Halloween pumpkins with markers. Love and fear seemed to be the root of her animosity now, but even with this recognition, I wasn't swayed in my thinking; I only began to grasp the space in which she brooded.

"Well guys, I think it's time to go," I said.

Jim had barely finished his meal but nodded his head in agreement. We left without singing "Happy Birthday" to him, without any cake, without his gifts, without my mother even coming to the door to say goodbye to us. After we walked outside and shut the car doors, Jim looked over at me.

"Nice job, Kel. What would make you think that your mom would be fine with this? Why would you bring it up tonight?"

"I don't know, Jim. I'm sorry. I don't know what I was thinking." I shook my head.

He was right; my timing was terrible. I had ruined the end of a nice Halloween night for my kids, and I had blown the celebration of his birthday. As we drove away, I considered what my mom's next step might be. Would she track down padlocks for my doors—or make a hysterical call to the Indian embassy? Both seemed in the realm of possibility.

FINDING BALANCE

I ALLOWED a few days to pass. Then I drove back to my parents' house in order to discuss the trip more freely with them. I knew it wouldn't be easy, but I hoped that my mom had cooled off. I stepped out of the car unhurriedly and walked onto their front porch, dodging the Halloween decorations that were still up. I felt like I was moving in slow motion, riding the escalator without taking a step and in no rush to meet whatever lay beyond my parents' front door.

My dad was sitting in his plaid recliner chair with his feet up when I walked in. He had on loose jeans, or "dungarees" as he called them, and a button-down shirt along with his infamous goggle-like glasses. Elton John would have been proud.

"Hi, Dad."

"Hi, Kel," he replied, staring at an open newspaper in his lap.

I did not stop to talk any further. I knew that I needed to speak with my mom first since she had been so angry with me. I walked upstairs and found my mom lying down in my brother's old room, reading a magazine. As I walked into the room, the creaky wooden floors gave her some indication that I had arrived, but she did not look up at me.

"Mom, this is the opportunity of a lifetime. I have the chance to learn about yoga and discuss all kinds of spiritual questions with wise teachers and people from all over the world. I could never do this here. I really feel like I need to go. Jim is completely behind me and this decision," I said, trying to sway her mind with Jim's support. "Plus, I'm going to get certified to teach hatha yoga, the physical yoga that they offer at different exercise places, and I might even be able to teach people when I get back home."

"You mean *if* you get back home." She began to shower me with a variety of scenarios that would require me to fly back, the mere thought of which, she hoped, would prevent me from even going. Then she squinted her eyes and pointedly asked, "Who is going to watch Kailee and Paige while you're away?"

"Jim, of course, and a lot of our friends who have offered to pitch in."

"Your *friends* are going to care for your children while you go to the other side of the world? What if they get sick? What if they're in an accident?"

"Mom, we're all going to be fine. Jim is here, and we have a lot of support."

"Well, I won't support you in any way," she said, sharply.

"Okay. Do you still want to pick up the girls after school on the days you're already doing it, before I leave?"

"I'll continue to pick them up from school, but they'll come to my house. You can pick them up on my porch because I don't want to see you."

I shook my head and felt disappointment arise, realizing that I couldn't put my children at risk of overhearing any more of my mom's feelings of aversion. "No thanks, Mom. I'll work something else out." I left the room, saying, "I'm going. I'm sorry you don't understand."

Throughout our entire discussion, I didn't feel any anger bubble up inside me. I knew that her feelings stemmed from a motherly and grandmotherly place of love. As a mother myself,

I wanted to believe that I would support my children if they ever felt drawn to something so deeply, but I also knew that I would voice my disagreement just as adamantly if I felt they were making a dangerous mistake. My mother never wanted me hurt, and in her eyes, this trip was too risky for me and for my children since I wouldn't be home to protect them. I also knew that I was still going.

On the way out, I stopped to talk with my dad. He put his newspaper down as I approached.

"Kelly, we live in a world filled with crazy people, terrorists. And you're purposely choosing to go to a place where you may be putting yourself in danger. You're leaving the safety and security of where we live and going somewhere—across the world—*by yourself*. I don't think it's a smart move."

"I understand what you're saying, Dad, and I'm sorry you don't agree. The world is a crazy place, but I'm not headed into nowhere land. I'm going to an ashram in India. I know the people I'll be staying with, and I know tons of people who have taken this same trip numerous times—and they're all fine. I'm really sorry that you and Mom don't understand, but I'm still going."

I ended the conversation there, assuming that he had already overheard all of my reasoning for taking the trip when I spoke with my mom. I walked over to him and kissed his head. Then I headed for the door. As I stepped back onto the front porch, I could almost hear my parents using the word "mother" in relation to me now but with a completely different connotation.

When I reached the car, I opened the door, sank into the seat, and stared at the familiar scenery in front of me. The rift between my parents and me seemed to extend beyond the borders of any international journey. Although I knew where my parents were coming from, I did not share their fears. I had accepted the fact that life is ultimately outside of anyone's control, and I held on to the idea that I could always fly back home if my family needed me. My parents could not grasp that this trip had begun to balance the needs I felt as mother, wife, and spiritual seeker—that nothing else filled the void I felt inside but this opportunity for growth. Staring at the swirling leaves in front of me, I was still resolved to set out, even though I had failed to garner their support. I felt as if I had just placed every chip on the table, and my heart had screamed, "All in."

28

AS THE CALENDAR moved closer to Thanksgiving, the supermarkets filled with turkeys and stuffing, but my relationship with my mom remained in the same place that it had been on Halloween night. She continued to hold on to her anger with me and my decision to go to India. We had not spoken to one another in weeks. Oddly, days before the holiday, my dad called. He used the phone as often as he traveled outside New York—rarely.

"Your mom is going to visit your aunt in Florida for Thanksgiving."

"Why? Is everything okay down there?" I asked, hoping for another reason for her trip other than circumvention.

"Everything is fine. She just said she wants to go. I'm not joining her," my dad responded, rather honestly.

"Okay, Dad. Well, if you're not doing anything, we'd love to have you over here on Thanksgiving. Ellie and Mike are coming over, too."

"Sounds good. Just tell me what time and what you'd like me to bring, and I'll be there."

"Just yourself. I'll get back to you on the time."

As I hung up the phone, my eyes filled with tears as I realized my mother wasn't only avoiding me now; she was fleeing the possibility of even seeing me.

On Thanksgiving Day, I watched Kailee and Paige prepare Thanksgiving dinner in their little plastic kitchen as I tended to the golden bird in our oven. After basting the turkey with rich pan drippings, I sauntered over to the girls' kitchen, opened their pink oven, and peered inside.

"Oh, your dinner looks delicious."

"Mom, don't let all the heat out. It's still cooking," the girls shouted.

"Sorry. Let me close this back up. Everyone will be here soon."

Hours later, the cranberry tablecloth disappeared under white platters and bowls filled with piping-hot stuffing, corn casserole, fresh, hot rolls, and golden brown turkey. My dad, Ellie, Mike, Jim, and our children sat around the table savoring the aromas and awaiting the go-ahead to begin. Jim looked over at my dad.

"So, Pops, would you like to say grace for us?"

"Sure," my dad said, amiably, as he clasped his hands together.

I looked above me, offering my own silent prayer, hoping that my dad's words would be short and sweet and pertain to the food and family around the table, without mention of any upcoming trip.

"Dear God," my father began. "We thank you for our family and friends. We thank you for this delicious food in front of us. And we are grateful for all of the time we get to spend together, laughing and enjoying each other's company. Amen."

"Amen," we responded.

Thank God, I silently offered above me, appreciating the succinctness of my dad's thoughtful words and hoping that my mom was wrapped in the same warmhearted feeling down South.

December brought forth its usual flurry of holiday shopping, decorating, and baking. In between trips to the mall and the food store, I finalized a five-week schedule of pickups, drop-offs, and play dates for Kailee and Paige. When I had met with Kim a couple of months before, she had given me some invaluable advice: "Just make sure that the couple of months preceding the trip aren't all about getting ready for it." I needed to be as efficient and clandestine as possible with all of my planning, engineering things behind the scenes like an Oscar-winning director—or good ol' Santa Claus.

As I ran into fellow moms and friends at different holiday gatherings, I was bombarded with mixed reactions. Sometimes I was met with, "Oh my God. That trip sounds amazing. I wish I could do something like that." Other times I heard, "Oh my God. I could never be away from my kids for that long—and never that far away." Of course, the latter made me feel like shit until I realized I probably would have said the same thing to someone else months before. I tried not to hold on to anything anyone said too tightly since it was more than enough just to contend with the discussions and feelings of my own family.

Days before Christmas, I prepared myself for the destruction of one of the most hallowed family traditions that Jim and I held. Since the girls had been babies, we began Christmas morning at home, usually at dawn's first light, under the boughs of a gaily decorated tree too big for our family room. After opening presents, we would head to my parents' house to open gifts there and share a delicious breakfast. Although I was ready to break from tradition and the annual trek to my parents' home, my phone rang with a surprise invitation a couple of days before the holiday.

"Hello," I said.

"Hi, Kelly. It's your mother."

"Hi, Mom," I replied, completely stunned.

"Well, I was just wondering if you, Jim, and the girls want to come over on Christmas morning to open up presents and have breakfast with us."

Holy shit. This is my early Christmas gift, I immediately thought.

"Yes, Mom. We'd love to. Maybe we can forget about India for Christmas."

"Okay, let's do that. Let's shelve it for now. But you're not going to drop another bomb on me while I'm cooking the sausage, are you?" she laughed.

"No, Mom. Definitely not. No more bombs in the kitchen. We're good."

"Then I'll see you after the kids wake up and open some presents at home."

"Great. See you around the crack of dawn," I replied, feeling childlike anticipation run through me.

On Christmas morning, we pulled into my parents' driveway bright and early. As we walked up the familiar steps of their home, I smelled bacon wafting outside. My dad had already opened the front door and was waiting to greet us on the porch.

"Merry Christmas!" he shouted, as clouds floated from his mouth in the frigid air.

"Merry Christmas!" we exclaimed.

"Merry Christmas. I love your pajamas, girls," my mom said, after we walked inside. She squeezed Kailee and Paige and kissed the tops of their heads.

I walked over to her and brought my arms around her, drawing in the familiar scent of her perfume. She reached back around me and drew me close, and I grew soft in the tender hold of her embrace. Moments later, we shifted our attention to two excited children.

"Girls, should we eat breakfast first or open gifts?" my mom asked, knowing their answer before she even asked the question.

"Presents!" they exclaimed.

"Of course," she laughed.

After we placed our gifts under the Christmas tree, Kailee and Paige donned elf hats and began passing them out. Giggling erupted as presents marked "Dad" went to Jim instead of my dad and vice-versa. Somehow the girls managed to get all of their gifts right, while my mom and I swapped presents with each other whenever we realized we were mistakenly handed a gift for the other "Mom." The air was light, and I realized how I missed my parents' company.

As I started opening one of my gifts, my mom looked over. The gift had an odd shape and felt pliable. I tore off the holiday wrapping paper, and my eyes filled with tears. Under the bright wrap was a Liz Claiborne piece of carry-on luggage. I started crying and so did my mom. I glanced over at my dad as he wiped his glassy eyes.

My parents didn't understand the need for my trip. They did not support it. That was clear. But they knew that I was going, and they wanted to show me that they loved me even when they wholeheartedly disagreed with me. I didn't want to let go of the bag. I did not want to open another thing. That piece of luggage held the love of my mother, my parents, inside it.

"Oh, Mom," I said.

"Merry Christmas, Kel," she replied through tears.

The rest of Christmas day was eventless—perfect. No bombshells dropped. No angry words shouted. Just lighthearted laughter and absolutely no talk of my upcoming trip.

I was scheduled to fly out on New Year's Eve. As that day grew closer, I reflected on the unpredictability of life. While I played with my children and Jim on the beach the previous summer, never would I have believed that I would be flying to an ashram in India within months—and on New Year's Eve no less. For the first time in my life, midnight on New Year's Eve would come without the company of my family—no sipping champagne, no kissing my husband or my young daughters.

On the night before my plane was to take off, my children sat on my bed as I tucked the last few items into my luggage.

"Just a few more things and I think I'm all packed," I said.

No one responded. Kailee forced a partial smile as I closed my suitcase. I walked over and drew both of my daughters close, smelling the sweet fragrance of shampoo lingering in their hair. Then I picked up a stack of different colored envelopes that I had stashed next to my bed. I handed the pile to Kailee and Paige and looked up at Jim who had entered the bedroom.

"I wrote a card for each of you, including you, Jim. There's one to open every day while I'm away."

The notes included jokes, riddles, games, and always an "I love you." I cried while I had written them out, alone under the dim lights of the local library while the girls jumped around in a gymnastic class a block away.

"I think I need a family hug," I said, gathering Kailee and Paige in my arms and feeling Jim reach around all of us.

Tears welled in my eyes, but I restrained them so that I wouldn't stir anyone else's water works. Somehow, we had found the strength to accept this five-week trip. But as the next day approached, five weeks away seemed as if it might last an eternity.

29

I REACHED OVER and turned my alarm off before I heard its familiar ring. I was lying in bed, hugging the edge since our family had decided to spend the night before my departure together—literally. Paige had managed to cocoon herself in all of the blankets, while Kailee had moved her growing body down to the bottom of the mattress to be less encumbered.

I smiled to myself as I gazed at my children's limber bodies relaxed in a sound sleep just as I had the morning before I shared the news about this trip. Maybe on some subconscious level, they were completely fine with this—in their hearts knowing that everything would be fine. Maybe this trip was easier to take than I had ever imagined. As I realized this would be my last view of them sleeping until I returned from India, I felt a twinge of sadness grab me. I knew that the next few hours would be a roller coaster of emotions.

Jim reached over Paige and lightly tapped my shoulder. As I turned to face him, he blew a kiss to me in the air, and I immediately blew one back. Within minutes, the girls woke up, and we snuggled together under the blankets that Paige readily shared. Before anyone started talking about the remainder of the day, I wiggled my fingers in the air.

"Oh no, I think my fingers are in need of some tickling." I pulled Paige toward me and worked my fingers around her belly.

"Mine too. I can't stop them from finding Kailee's arm pits." Jim reached down to the bottom of the bed and yanked Kailee toward the top.

Within minutes, the covers were on the floor, and all of us were laughing out loud. We cuddled together for a bit longer, and then Jim headed downstairs to make a light breakfast for us. I rolled out of bed and finished packing some last minute items and noticed that the girls had begun watching my every move. The next few hours were a blur as we tried to laugh and joke about anything other than my departure. Then the dreaded moment of separation arrived.

"I know, guys. I can't believe the time is already here either," I said, as I gathered Kailee and Paige in my arms.

Jim walked over and brought his arms around all of us. As I felt the blanket of his embrace, I realized how strong his arms were, how strong he really was. I knew that he would hold on tightly to our girls while I was away, but I was starting to feel my own reluctance in letting any of this go. I closed my eyes, reassuring myself that I would be surrounded by friends and Guruji soon, and I would be back here in no time. Deep down, I knew that I was ready to embark on this adventure. I slowly released my hold on my family and gave them a slight smile as I reached for another tissue.

"I'll be back before you know it," I offered, wiping my nose.

As if she didn't hear me, Kailee asked, "Mom, can I have that tissue in your hand?"

"Sure," I said, grimacing. "Thanks for throwing it out for me."

"No, Mom," Paige interjected. "We aren't throwing your tissues away. You won't be here for a while, so we want to keep everything of yours."

Before I could respond, Kailee added, "Yeah Mom, even your dead tissues. We're keeping these. They're staying in this bowl until you get back home."

A piece of my heart broke off as I realized my children weren't even able to let go of my used tissues now. *How will they be able to let go of me momentarily?*

"Well, if they start to look gross, you have my permission to get rid of them and replace them with new tissues."

"No, Mom, they're staying right here," Paige said, rather firmly, picking up the bowl.

We laughed a little, very little, and talked about staying in touch via email and telephone. Since the ashram's computer system in India was going through some changes, we weren't sure if we would have the capability to communicate through video while I was away. With or without live streaming, the girls had ascertained ways of making me feel their colorful presence in India. They picked up a manila envelope and withdrew hand-drawn pictures.

"Mom, you can put these in your room at the ashram," Paige said, her wide eyes glimmering.

"They are beautiful. Thank you, girls."

I rubbed my daughters' wet, red cheeks. Then Kailee and Paige watched as I tucked the pictures alongside the pink travel blanket and pillow they had also given me for the trip. I closed my Liz Claiborne carry-on bag and wrapped my arms around my family.

Within minutes, our friend Mike arrived. He was my chauffeur for the start of this journey and had offered to take me to the ashram where I would hook up with another transport to the airport. Mike knew our family well and wanted to ease this initial departure in whatever way he could.

"I think it's almost time to go," he said, placing his hand on my shoulder.

I knelt down and hugged and kissed Kailee and Paige individually. Then I drew Jim close. As I followed Mike out the door and looked back at my family, I saw that Paige had already climbed into Jim's arms, and he was breaking one arm free to draw it around Kailee. I snapped a picture in my mind and knew that I would look back on this moment countless times.

Mike and I arrived at the ashram a short time later. My new traveling partner, Annie, was already loading her suitcase into the back of a van when we pulled in.

Annie was an old friend from the ashram and was heading to the retreat on the same flight as me. She was a petite woman in her early fifties. Her long black hair had natural wisps of gray winding through it, and she wore it tied back in a loose braid. I smiled and noticed that Annie and I had both dressed comfortably in light capris for our lengthy trip, and her makeup matched her outfit, soft and unassuming; it was barely noticeable. I waved to her as I stepped out of Mike's truck, and she made a beeline over to me, greeting me with a hug.

"It's so great to see you. I'm so glad we'll be traveling together."

"Me too, Annie. Hard to believe we'll be on the other side of the world soon."

I followed Mike to the back of his truck and reached for the handle of one of my bags. As I did so, Mike turned to me and grabbed hold of my shoulders.

"Be careful—seriously." The unsaid words running through his mind were probably something more like, *"If I wasn't sure airport security would confiscate them, I would load you up with a rifle, bullets, a machete, a bow and arrow, and possibly a few bodyguards."* Aloud, he added, "Be safe."

"I will, Mike. I will." I hugged him and whispered, "You watch out for my girls and Jim."

When I looked back at him, he smiled and nodded, and I knew that he would be the perfect security system for my family. I could not have left them in better hands.

Annie and I arrived at the airport early and had a few moments to grab something to eat before we boarded the plane.

"What are you in the mood for, Annie? Even though I think I could go for a nice salami sandwich, I think I have to start bridging my eating habits toward the ashram's vegetarian menu."

"Smart plan, Kel," she laughed.

Moments later, we sat down at a booth with our veggie burgers and fries and talked about everything, except for my family. I wasn't ready or able to talk about them without crying, and I was unsure whether I would have the strength to do so at any point during my time away. We intentionally kept our conversation on the lighter side of the force, in the neighborhood of bubblegum and rainbows.

When it was time to board the plane, I discreetly reached into my Liz Claiborne bag, twisted off the top of a pill container, and popped a small anxiety-reducing drug. I wanted to ensure a relaxing, eventless trip as my physical body left my dearest loves thousands of miles behind. After I boarded the plane and sat down in my assigned seat, I reached back into my bag and withdrew a book that I thought would lead to a few hours of deep, dreamless sleep.

But a woman seated near me had other plans. This beautiful stranger opened up to me like I was the sole bartender in an empty bar. She was in love with someone other than her husband and was en route to see him. She had children and knew that she would never be able to be with the love of her life because of family and societal pressures. Her lover was from another caste in India.

Although I had wanted my spiritual hiatus to begin the moment I sat on my airplane seat, fate had other things in store for me. I contemplated my marriage—where Jim and I had been, how far we had come, how lucky I was to be taking this trip knowing that my children were in safe hands. I listened to this beautiful woman, felt her pain, and offered whatever solace I could muster.

New Year's Eve always seems like the perfect time to look back on the previous year and contemplate resolutions for the new one. This New Year's Eve was no different. I had already considered where my marriage had been and where we were headed, and now I was flying across the globe, already resolved to reaffirm my spiritual footing and about to study yoga as I had never done before. Physically, my world had done a 180-degree turn—with a clear landing almost certain, barring any unforeseen airplane trouble. However, mentally, emotionally, spiritually—in every other way—I was in motion, and my landing would take time to decipher.

IV
GROUNDED IN MOTHER INDIA

FINDING BALANCE

THE PLANE touched down in India smoothly. I peered out the window, trying to get my first glimpse of the new country I would be calling home for the next few weeks. Night had taken hold, and all I could decipher were the red and green airport lights that surrounded the runway. I looked over at Annie and mouthed, "Yay," as I gently clapped my hands, feeling both relief and excitement take hold.

After we grabbed our carry-on bags and retrieved the rest of our luggage from inside the terminal, we looked around until we spotted a young Indian man holding a sign with the name of our destination on it. Another couple who shared our stop was already standing next to our driver. We dashed over and introduced ourselves. Our English was met with smiles and limited responses from the couple who had come from Mexico and from our Hindi or Gujarati or Marathi speaking driver. We shared enough verbal conversation and impromptu sign language to know that we were in the right place and with the right people.

As we walked outside the airport and into the balmy Indian evening, I drew in a deep breath and embraced my new surroundings. *I'm really here*, I thought, rejoicing inside. Then we piled our luggage into the back of a timeworn van and headed toward the ashram. Halfway into the ride, our driver pulled into a parking lot in front of a long, open trailer. Large, window-like openings on its side displayed bags of unfamiliar snacks, rolls of candy, fresh fruit, and cans of drinks.

In English, the driver said, "We will take a break. Use the bathroom or buy something to eat." Annie looked over at me, and I shook my head *No*.

"I have no idea what I'd be buying, and I don't want to risk feeling uncomfortable, belly-wise, in this van," I said, grimacing.

"You're right. But I need to use the bathroom."

As Annie and I walked to the public restrooms, we noticed something on the ground. From a distance, it looked like a small, sleeping animal, maybe a possum. As we grew closer, we realized it was a huge, dead rat right in the middle of our path. I stood there, paralyzed for a moment, immediately thinking, *Holy shit. Will this be my life for the next five weeks?* Then Annie's eyes met mine, and we cautiously stepped around the dead rodent and up the stairs that led to the bathroom.

After I came out of the stall, I unconsciously washed my hands in the public faucet. As a mom, I'm unbelievably aware of wipes of all kinds, hand sanitizer, antibacterial soap, and just about every known cleaning agent. And I generally have them stashed everywhere—in my pocketbook, my car, my pockets, my bra—wherever necessary. But, unfortunately for me, as soon as my feet touched ground in India, all of my antibacterial, motherly, cleaning smarts left me.

From behind me, I heard Annie say, "Kelly, you didn't just rinse your hands in that faucet, did you?"

Time stood still, and I froze, thinking, *Oh shit. I've been here for less than two hours and I've just poured India's non-filtered water into every pore.* Our next stop will likely be at an Indian hospital where I will be barfing my brains out. *"Be safe. Watch yourself. Be careful."* All of the warnings from my family and friends ran through my mind a little too late. Annie whipped out her hand sanitizer, and I infused it into my entire body. Nothing could have lived—no bacteria, no fungus, no rare Indian disease. My skin barely hung on.

"Thank you, Annie. What the hell was I thinking?"

"I have no idea. Maybe you weren't thinking. It's so easy to do things automatically, but we can't right now."

"You're right. Thanks for saving my ass so soon, from one mother to another."

Annie smiled as we headed back around the dead rat and into the waiting van. After I shut the door, our driver pulled back onto the road, darting between trucks, motorcycles, cars, bikes, whatever, at lightning speed and within inches of the back or side of a moving vehicle. I clenched my teeth and squeezed the edge of the seat. I had driven in New York City countless times and felt the relentless push to keep moving, but the traffic in India seemed beyond any of that.

"Maybe this is where New York taxi drivers get their training," I whispered to Annie.

She smiled and nodded her head as the van swerved to the right, and my body veered into hers. I closed my eyes and drew myself off of my friend, grateful that I hadn't bought anything to eat at our last stop.

A few hours later, our van slowed as it followed a long white concrete wall leading to a sturdy wooden gate where we were waved in. It was around three in the morning, and we had arrived at the ashram. Our driver stopped so that we could get our room assignments and further directions. Then our van continued toward our rooms, and I tried to get a feel for the place around me. Unfortunately, I couldn't see much in the dark night. The road that we were driving on felt bumpy, so I assumed it was probably made of dirt—or dead rats—and hopefully not the latter. All I could make out were shadowy trees interspersed between buildings and paths. Annie and I were driven to a three-story building that looked similar to a large motel, with numerous doors dotting long open hallways.

As I stepped out of the van, I took a deep breath. The still night air was warm and had the slightest fragrance of rich tropical flowers. Annie grabbed her luggage from the back of the van and headed to her room. I took hold of mine and walked in a different direction, up two stories of concrete steps. I knocked at a door on the second floor and waited with anticipation to see who my new roommate would be for the next five weeks. A moment later, the door opened, and I recognized the smiling face immediately.

"Welcome to India," the blue-eyed woman beamed.

"Beth, it's so great to see you," I exclaimed.

"I'm so glad you're here. Annie and Kathy are roommates on the first floor of this building."

"Oh, perfect. I'm glad that we're all so close."

Beth was an acquaintance from the ashram in New York. Although we didn't know each other well, I was grateful to be rooming with someone familiar. Beth took one of the bags from my hands and led me inside our room. Even though it was the middle of the night, she seemed wide awake; her short, highlighted hair seemed perfectly in place as it framed her face. Her powder blue pajamas hung casually from her body, and the comfort they exuded made me yearn for my own.

As I glanced around our room, I noticed two twin beds, fully made, with a folded, gray blanket at the foot of each. A wooden nightstand sat beside each bed. The floor was marble or a smooth, hard stone that I took to be marble, and a bathroom and shower lay beyond an open archway. I had expected very little in terms of my room and was met with abundance. It was more beautiful than

I had ever expected.

"I hope you had an easy trip. Kathy and I flew in together a few days ago."

"That was smart. It gave you guys a few days to get used to the time change before the yoga course begins."

"Yes. I'm still not totally in the groove with the change in day and night, but I feel better than the first day. You'll get used to it."

Although I could have taken an earlier flight, I had not wanted to put the burden of a few extra days away on my family; Annie and I had twenty-four hours to become acclimated to our new setting before the course began. Before Beth slid under her blanket, she offered a quick update on the activities that were to begin in a few short hours. Then she stretched out and closed her eyes, and I headed to the bathroom to wash up and slip into my pajamas. Moments later, I lay down on my bed, closed my eyes, and drifted off to sleep easily.

FINDING BALANCE

31

IT SEEMED LIKE my head had just hit the pillow when I heard the chime of my cell phone's alarm. I rose slowly and walked to the open window to survey my surroundings. The night sky was still out since it was the wee hours of the morning, but I was able to discern the tall trees and leafy bushes with more clarity and saw the first rumblings of movement on the dirt paths. I couldn't wait to dive into my surroundings more fully.

I opened up my suitcase and hunted for a pair of tan leggings and a big, white, cotton shirt that had a subtle swirly design sewn into the fabric. Over the years, I had picked up a few loose tunics that seemed to fit the Indian motif I was trying to blend into. Then I dug a bit deeper in search of my pink wool shawl, knowing that it would brighten my outfit and offer some warmth. Since I was unsure of the weather, I planned to dress in layers. After I placed my clothing on the bed, I grabbed my towel and sat down, patiently waiting for the shower. Flickers of excitement ran through me as I anticipated the day. A few moments later, Beth walked out of the bathroom and back into the bedroom.

"Good morning," she said.

"Good morning," I replied, as I walked passed her and into the bathroom. "I still can't believe I'm here."

"I know. I'm still getting used to it, too."

As I turned and closed the heavy curtain that partitioned the bathroom from the bedroom, I knew that I wasn't fully awake yet. My body craved a strong cup of coffee. I stepped into the shower and prayed for warm water. I turned the knob, and tepid water sprinkled down. I began to feel gratitude for the smallest of things.

After the shower, I dressed quickly. Since I was unsure of the time and didn't see a clock, I decided to forgo the mascara and liner and go *au naturel*. Beth was waiting for me so that we could walk to the temple together for the morning chant, and I didn't want to risk making us late.

"Thanks for waiting," I said, as I walked back into the bedroom.

"Of course, so glad you're here. It's really beautiful. You're going to love it."

We walked out of our room and down the concrete steps of our building. A moment later, our feet touched a dirt path leading to the temple. I drew in the sweet perfume of the surrounding blossoms, just as I had a few hours earlier upon my arrival, and I scanned the green vegetation around me. Even though the sun had not come up yet, the ashram grounds still looked lush.

A minute later, we were standing in front of the temple and the familiar scent of incense was swirling through the air. A large, golden statue of a familiar Indian saint, seated with crossed legs, sat against the far wall facing us, while more colorful statues dwarfed his sides. The wall behind the statues was decorated with colorful streams of fabric that billowed from the ceiling to the earth. The other three sides of the temple consisted of a half wall or no wall, and giant poles on the periphery held up the roof. The openness of the temple allowed me to continue to view the rich ashram grounds, which had once been an entire mango orchard.

Beth and I removed our shoes and placed them on handmade wooden shelves before walking inside. The ground inside the temple felt hard under my feet and was only softened slightly by the beige and orange rugs that covered it. We walked to the center of the temple and sat cross-legged on the ground near Kathy and Annie, who had arrived earlier. Men sat on one side of the temple and women sat on the other, an ancient tradition I had grown accustomed to during my time spent at ashrams in New York. As I looked around, I noticed a few elderly people seated in a row of chairs that faced the statues. Their eyes were closed, and they looked as still as the carved figures before us.

When I heard the familiar tune of the mantra begin, I began to chant as if I had always been there. I did not feel like a guest at the ashram. I didn't feel like this was my first time sitting on the ground in a temple in India. I felt comfortable, as if I were surrounded by family at a distant relative's home. I felt like I was supposed to be there.

After the chant ended in the main temple, breakfast was served. Quietly, my friends and I followed a dirt path over to the dining hall together. It was still early, and I wasn't sure if our silence stemmed from our own drowsiness or from the calm that the temple and the ashram exuded. The hall was only a short walk away, and I was amazed at its openness. It was unlike any other dining area I had ever seen. It consisted of a long, open, cemented floor that was covered by a roof, held up by strategically placed poles.

Since most people sat on the ground to eat, there were only two oversized wooden tables with chairs available. Kathy, Annie, Beth, and I decided to share our first meal together at one of the empty tables. We put our bags and shawls on some chairs and then stood in line for the homemade breakfast being served. The air smelled like white rice or oatmeal, and as I peeked my head around the line, I spotted a young boy dishing yellow squares sprinkled with black seeds into thin bowls made of leaves.

Kathy turned to me and said, "*Dhokla*. Delicious."

I smiled and remembered that I had this meal at the ashram in New York numerous times. It was made from chickpea or rice flour, I thought, and was often served with chopped cilantro. I took my bowl from the hands of a young Indian boy.

"Thank you," I said. He smiled and nodded. I grasped a cup of hot chai from the hands of another young Indian boy. Again I said, "Thank you."

This time, the boy replied, "You're most welcome." His English was a pleasant surprise. I knew that many of the people involved in the yoga retreat would be speaking English, but it would be a wait-and-see game with others.

My friends and I sat down at our table and were joined by other individuals who, I soon found out, were taking the yoga course as well, including the Mexican couple who Annie and I arrived with a few hours earlier. Thankfully, most spoke English, with accents from around the globe. After we shared some good morning pleasantries, I looked around for the silverware.

"Kel, you can ask someone for a spoon or just use your hands to eat," Kathy said. "Either way is totally fine."

I nodded my head and considered the choice. Then I picked up a soft, spongy square of *dhokla* with my hands and took a bite. *If only Kailee and Paige could see me now*, I thought to myself, recalling all of the times I had reminded my own children to use their forks or spoons—and not their hands—while eating. My head was giving way to my heart, and I was beginning to embrace the fullness that even a simple meal could invoke when eaten with my hands. I was feeling my food through almost every sense—taste, feel, smell, and sight—and beginning to live more mindfully.

"Do you think I could go up and get another cup of chai?" I asked my friends.

"Definitely," Kathy replied. "As long as there's still some left."

I walked back to the breakfast line and was handed another cup of chai. As I returned to the table, I brought the tea to my face to draw in its' sweet aroma. I relished every part of my hot drink, knowing that the caffeine and my excitement on this first day were responsible for keeping my body vertical after only a few hours of sleep.

Once breakfast was over, my friends and I stepped onto a winding dirt path and began our own self-guided tour. Young boys, who looked between the ages of seven to twenty, walked with notebooks in hand along the dirt paths and in and out of different buildings.

"These are some of the students from the Sanskrit school that's run here for boys. Many of them have been saved from tragic misfortune just by coming here," Kathy shared. "In one case, a father brought his seven-year-old son to the ashram because his wife had died, and he had to work. There was no one—no school, no family, no government program, nothing—to look after his young boy while he worked. He was desperate for someone to help. And luckily for him, the ashram took the boy in and enrolled him as a student."

"Jesus, that's awful and yet amazing," I said. "Our kids are so lucky."

"Yes, you're right," Beth agreed. "And most times, they don't even realize how lucky they are."

Kathy nodded her head and continued. "All of the students in the Sanskrit school reside here at the ashram and head home, if there is one to go to, during school breaks."

Since I knew that the ashram schedule could be chock full of activities, I hoped that the lives of the young boys wouldn't just be jammed with learning Sanskrit and chanting 24-7. I wanted them to have time to play and enjoy their childhood, too. Moments later, we passed by a group of boys laughing and joking around in a grassy field. They were playing cricket (similar to baseball but with an odd, flat bat and only two bases, or so I gathered). Relief surged through my body.

"The gift shop is just ahead," Kathy noted. "Let's go in and browse. They have such beautiful things there."

We came across the short, one-story, concrete building in an instant. After I walked through the wooden door, I was stunned by all of the brilliantly colored items surrounding me. Jewel-toned bags embellished with silver and gold thread hung from racks, and multi-colored blankets and religious statues rested on tables. Saris made of exquisite silks and satins hung from the walls. Ornate rugs, handcrafted wall hangings, and luxurious shawls were sprawled throughout the room. My eyes danced in the rich rainbow of colors around me.

"The ashram started a business a couple of years ago and taught the women from nearby villages how to sew. Now they're able to support their families," Beth said, picking up a satiny magenta pouch. "They've made almost everything here."

"Wow. That's awesome," I said.

I allowed my hands to linger on the sequined handbags and silky shirts. All of the items were unique, and now I knew that by purchasing them, I was helping other women support their own children and contributing to the ashram in some way. I felt a deeper connection to some larger community, outside even the walls of the ashram.

As we continued strolling the grounds, we met our yoga teachers and many of our soon-to-be fellow classmates. People from Australia, New Zealand, Mexico, Europe, all over, came to this little ashram in India. As I looked around, the love and peace were almost palpable.

For the remainder of the day, my friends and I met and chatted with other people who had come for the yoga retreat. We shared an afternoon chant and lunch together. We enjoyed dinner and an evening chant in the main temple. We began to get to know each other beyond the opening lines, "Hi. How are you? Nice to meet you," and I started relaxing into my surroundings. When the day's activities and conversation ended, we headed back to our respective rooms to rest.

After I settled into my room that evening, physical exhaustion engulfed my body. I needed sleep. I was living in a completely different time zone. India was approximately ten and a half hours ahead of New York time, so India's day was actually New York's night and vice versa. In the silence of my room, I was also beginning to miss my family. I looked over at the colored pictures that Kailee and Paige had given to me that now rested on my bedside table. My eyes filled with tears, and I closed my eyes. *Everyone is fine, and I just need to sleep*, I reminded myself. After a full day of meeting new people, exploring new places, chanting, chatting, and feeling some ease, I went into a deep sleep that carried me into the light of my first day of the yoga retreat, my first day of school.

FINDING BALANCE

32 I WOKE TO THE RING of my cell phone alarm at 5:15am on the first day of the retreat. As my heavy eyelids opened, I noticed that Beth had already showered. I had not heard her stir; she had flowed through the room with the subtlety of a light breeze. I moved slowly toward the shower and then meandered down the dirt path to the main temple. The morning was still dark, and the stars continued to poke through the black sky.

Within moments, I was seated behind the open walls of the temple, and my voice joined with others chanting mantras. Soon, the sun began to rise. It was almost as if the brilliant star waited for our song to draw it up from the horizon. As it rose, it gave everything around us a pinkish, golden hue.

I closed my eyes and allowed myself to sing freely with the voices around me. Unlike at home, I didn't feel a need to open my eyes and check on what my children were doing or retrieve my cell phone to ensure that no one needed me. No one tapped my leg or whispered something in my ear. Effortlessly, my mind, body, and spirit dove into the stillness that my surroundings offered.

After the morning chant ended, I ate breakfast in the open

dining hall with my friends. We savored hot chai and warm *dosas*, Indian style pancakes, with coconut chutney and potatoes stewed in aromatic spices. Then we strolled to our first yoga class together.

Our classroom was nearby, in a one-story building on the ashram grounds. Once inside, I took a seat on a thin, caramel-colored rug that lay on top of a concrete floor, and I began to appreciate the simplicity of the room. A small ceramic vase holding red hibiscus flowers rested on a table next to a framed picture of Guruji. Other pictures of gurus from this lineage hung on the walls. The view of the flourishing grounds through the bare, open windows offered the only other decoration.

Twenty-five students, ranging in age from their twenties to their seventies and from all over the world, joined me. Some sat on the floor, while others rested on chairs. Our instructors sat on the earth at the far end of the room and began our first class with a short chant. Then we moved our seats into a circle and were asked to introduce ourselves to the group by sharing our reason for coming to India and joining in this yoga retreat.

As we confided in one another, I began to feel our unity. A thread was being sewn from one individual to the next; our stories were completely different and completely the same. I cried along with my fellow classmates while we listened to and shared some of our deepest feelings, reasons for coming, and reasons for being. As I listened to each person's story, I felt the love and acceptance in the room. I had never been a part of anything like this before. I was the last person to share in our circle of students. I was the latch on the necklace, connecting one end to the other.

"Hi. I'm Kelly. I'm from New York. I have a loving husband and two beautiful children at home—two girls, Kailee and Paige. I miss them very much, but I'm also so glad to be here. For some reason, I felt this need to know more...more about yoga...more about this path...more about myself...just plain more. I always knew that I wanted to come to India at some point in my life, especially with one of my close friends, and time and opportunity allowed many things to fall into place for me so this could happen. Besides this inner thirst for this experience, I'm not one hundred percent clear as to why I'm here at this exact moment in time. I don't know what the grand plan is yet."

"And maybe there isn't a grand plan right now," one of my instructors offered. "Maybe you're just supposed to be right here, in this moment, right now."

"Yes, maybe. I don't know. I'm definitely going to try to stay in the moment and not let my head go to my kids, my home, or anywhere else because I know I'm so lucky to be here. I miss my family, but I'm still really glad that I'm here, meeting all of you and about to study yoga together."

I ended my introduction there and considered what my instructor had shared. Remaining focused and present seemed like the perfect plan to savor each day and to prevent homesickness from taking hold. I couldn't allow my mind to dwell on being thousands of miles away from my family for five weeks; I needed to find a way to savor this sweet space with my new friends. I turned my attention back toward my instructor and listened as he transitioned our discussion to the roots of yoga philosophy.

After the first class ended, we took a short break. I walked the grounds and strolled around the dirt paths. I couldn't get over how lush the property was—mango trees, vivid pink and marmalade-colored flowers, lime green bushes and grass. Wasn't India supposed to be dry and hot? It seemed I had unknowingly come to this spiritual paradise during the perfect season. It wasn't too wet, too dry, too hot, or too cold. I felt like Goldilocks enjoying Baby Bear's perfect things.

The remainder of the day included lunch, a hatha yoga class, time for chai and casual conversation, another chant, dinner, and an evening program. After dinner, my busy day caught up with me. I had spent numerous hours traveling, only a few hours sleeping, and a great deal of time getting acclimated to my new setting. That night, I needed to crash. All of the talk about my children and husband during that first class and on breaks with new friends kept them forefront in my mind. I had heard their voices upon arrival when I called home to confirm my safe landing, and our emails throughout the day had allowed their words to linger. My physical exhaustion coupled with their absence led to a mini-emotional breakdown that evening.

While Beth went to the evening program, I decided that I needed to stay in our room alone and try to sleep, as well as release a few thousand tears. I wanted to sleep but was overtired. I lay in my twin bed, dark room, a gazillion miles away from my daughters and husband and cried; I missed them so much. As the sacred words from the chant began drifting through my open window, I tried to follow them in my mind but found that I was too tired for that, yet not tired enough to sleep. There was nothing in my room to draw my attention away from thoughts of my family. No television to watch. No radio to listen to. I felt my pillow becoming drenched in tears.

I glanced at my bedside table, and my eyes caught hold of the homemade pictures that the girls had made for me. My eyes became blurry with tears again after I read the colored "I love you Mom" written on top. In the back of my mind, I knew that I could always go home if I needed to, but I also knew that I needed to give myself more time at the ashram to see if the next day or so would get any easier. Like a dip in frigid water, I knew that the potential existed for my environment to become more palatable with time—if I could only remain immersed, endure this initial discomfort, and keep swimming.

I had stopped crying by the time Beth walked into our room

after the evening program ended. I must have looked beyond tired, with worn-out, red eyes, the kind I used to get from spending time with tequila drinking friends.

"I hope you got some sleep," Beth whispered.

"What did I miss?" I asked, trying to smile.

"Guruji asked all of the people from our retreat to share why we had come to India and what we hoped to get out of our time here. Luckily, we had already shared some of this during class so part of the response was already in our heads. Then we chanted. I think there were probably about seventy other people there tonight, including the Sanskrit students, their teachers, and some other ashram residents."

A small piece of me was sorry to have missed the program, but a larger piece of me was glad that I did. I felt like fate had just dealt me a royal flush. Had I gone to the temple and been asked to share anything aloud, my emotions and exhaustion probably would have overcome me, leading me to respond like a giant emotional hot mess. But since I stayed in, I only had my own tears and thoughts to swim in—without the audience.

I didn't share my own evening program of heartache with my new roommate because I knew that I would have started crying again. Beth would have surely hugged me and that would have allowed me to melt into her arms and lose every bit of the strength I had mustered before she arrived. When I finally let go of all thought, all emotion, and gave in to my exhaustion, I fell asleep. I don't even remember dreaming that night, only waking to the sound of my cell phone alarm before the sun touched the horizon.

FINDING BALANCE

33

I WAS TIRED as I climbed out of bed but not exhausted. I felt like I needed a fresh start. I stepped into the shower and let the warm water wash away the salty remnants of the previous night's sea of tears. After I dressed, I began the familiar walk down the dirt path to the temple. I gazed up at the stars that were still out and drew in the early morning air. Then I tightened the wrap of my pink shawl and sat down in the temple among old and new friends. I closed my eyes and begged the universe, *Please let this day be easier.*

A few moments later, my mind slipped into the melodious words of the chant, and any thoughts of the previous evening floated away. My attention remained inside the temple like the smoky incense hanging above my head, and when the chant ended, I opened my eyes slowly and felt at peace.

I walked to the dining area and chatted casually with friends over breakfast. Then I headed to class and allowed my mind to become occupied with the subjects offered in the open, sacred space of the concrete classroom. My heart began to loosen its strings to home. My love and yearning to hug and kiss my children and husband didn't leave, but those feelings took an accepting back seat to my desire to stay at the ashram. I began to feel hopeful that my journey away from my family would get easier.

The schedule for the rest of the afternoon was much like the day before. Chanting, hatha yoga, and yoga philosophy were integral pieces. These components continued to frame the following days, and I found comfort in their routine. The steady menu of courses also allowed the rich discussion from one class to carry over to the next. I felt myself flowing with the schedule, moving through the workshops and then through each day with greater ease.

During the course of the day, chanting offered the invitation for all of our distinct voices to meld into a single one each time we came together in song. Although we sang repeatedly, I never grew tired of it. It almost had some *Kumbaya* effect, linking everyone to one another, to the One, to our spirit; when we joined in a chant, I felt a unity that went beyond our voices.

Every afternoon, we were guided into different *asanas*, or postures, in a hatha yoga class. These classes took place under the shelter of a concrete roof and behind half walls that allowed the outside in. I stared at leafy mango trees firmly rooted in the earth while I tried to maintain my own footing in each new stretch.

At least twice a day, we came together within the walls of a classroom to delve into yoga philosophy, contemplating being both human and divine—and how that could even be possible. We learned about different Hindu traditions and *Ayurveda*, the healing and healthy living practices used in India often referred to as the *Science of Life*. We delved into ancient yogic stories and teachings and discussed their meanings and application in our own world.

We talked about what it means to live in this world and also be detached. Detachment didn't refer to disengaging from loved ones or dropping out of life but rather living fully with the capacity to let things go. It alluded to an underlying acceptance of the way life unfolds and an ability to move forward without clinging to the past or to any future desire.

I struggled to understand how detachment could be realized by someone like me, someone so attached to her family. My role as a mom seemingly clouded any remote possibility of parting from anyone or with anything. Even in moments like this, without my family beside me, I still felt completely attached to them. I couldn't imagine a time when my heart wouldn't beat in unison with theirs, racing a mile a minute when something exciting happened or skipping a beat if tragedy struck. The notion of moving forward regardless of circumstance seemed inconceivable. What if Kailee or Paige became extremely sick? What if my children, or my husband, or someone I loved was terribly hurt— or died? Could I ever just continue on? I wanted to imbibe the peace that a sense of detachment offered in all of life's twists and turns, but I wondered whether that was realistic in my world.

Sitting alone under the umbrella of a wooden roof in a small, open temple on the edge of the ashram grounds, I contemplated…and an understanding washed over me. Maybe detachment wasn't something that I could readily bring into my life at will. Perhaps it would arise naturally as I lived with the understanding that the ultimate outcome of my choices—the ultimate outcome of my children's choices, my husband's choices, everyone's choices—is in the hands of some greater universal force. Faith in that universal force might lead me to that place of detachment, where I could let go because I accepted that everything in life happens for a reason—that divine wisdom ultimately throws the final card, that there really is perfection in the seeming imperfect. If I lived with that understanding, I might be able to revel in a moment, a person, a thing and then be able to let go of it all if circumstances changed.

I recalled an insight that a teacher at the ashram in New York once shared at a retreat: *"There are many who ask why things happen or why we are here. Some come to a place where there is no 'why.' There just 'is.'"* They come to a place of acceptance when they are ready and let go of their questions. I surmised that all answers and all sense of detachment may ultimately reside in faith—and I would grasp all when I was ready. I couldn't force unnatural feelings or ways of being upon myself, even if I saw the value in them. The fruits of this path would show themselves as I dove more deeply into my faith, and like the waves of the ocean, a deeper sense of commitment to my spiritual journey washed over me.

Over the next few weeks, our instructors guided our discourse down myriad roads, and my mind remained focused on the subjects contemplated in the classroom. Due to the melting pot of cultures and generations present, each lesson and conversation had its own unique and thoughtful feel. Every participant in class shared their thoughts and understandings freely, adding their own spice to the rich stew of discussion. My mind savored the different tastes in every philosophic exchange. Often I found myself sitting alone in the modest temple, under the wooden roof, pondering topics from class—life, death, one's purpose. As I allowed my mind and heart to explore the tangible and intangible, each day left a different impression inside me.

The only day when tranquility left me and I longed to be home was Kailee's birthday. When that day arrived, I couldn't wait to call her. Since I was living half a day ahead of New York time, I had to calculate the timing of my call so that everyone would surely be together and awake—and that meant that I had to rely on my friends and the retreat schedule to keep my mind and body busy for hours until it was time to make the call.

After the morning chant ended, I ran from the temple, dodged up the concrete steps of my building, and unlocked the door of my room in lightning speed. I tossed my shawl on the bed and rummaged feverishly through my bag for my cell phone. Unfortunately, as soon as I heard Kailee's voice over the phone, I felt the physical distance between us in light years.

"Happy birthday to you," I sang, as tears filled my eyes. "Happy birthday to you," I stammered. My throat began to close slightly as I tried to hold back a sob. "Sorry Kai. I have a tickle in my throat." I swallowed hard and tried to pull myself together.

"That's okay, Mom. We're at Aunt Ellie and Uncle Mike's house right now."

"Oh wow. That's so great." I pulled the phone away from my face, sniveling, feeling the tears welling in my eyes again.

"Mom, Uncle Mike even made my favorite cake for me."

"Vanilla with sprinkles inside?"

"Yup. It's going to be delicious."

"I'm sure it will be. Mike is a pretty big hunter, Kai, but I didn't realize he baked, too. You must be pretty special. Maybe I'll have to get him to bake something for me when I get back."

"Yeah, Mom. Maybe some cupcakes."

My feelings lifted. She sounded okay, I realized. Unlike me, she wasn't holding back cries. She was wrapped in the arms of friends and family in New York, and she sounded just fine. I was filled with such a gigantic mesh of feelings—love, longing, sadness, gratitude. Just as my friends in India had supported me earlier in the day, our friends at home were doing the same for my family. We had all been swathed in a cocoon of love, and thankfully, that was all I needed to understand to deter any purchase of an early plane ticket home. Supportive surroundings had been the key for everyone—along with a sweet, speckled piece of cake for Kailee.

"Well, my little ten-year-old," I said, after briefly speaking with everyone, "enjoy your special cake and the rest of your birthday. I can't wait to celebrate with you when I get home."

"Me too, Mom."

"I love you," I said. I hung up the phone and allowed myself to let go of the day, just like I let go of her hand on the first day of kindergarten.

After Kailee's birthday passed, I began to swim more easily in the serenity of the ashram. In the peaceful space that I savored, I became even more contemplative. I took time to ponder my existence as mother, wife, daughter, sister, person. I sat alone in the temple embracing the peace and stillness. I walked the ashram grounds—smelling the wild flowers, observing the verdant mango trees and emerald green bushes. I pondered gratitude—for my children, my husband, my family, my friends, my time at the ashram. I pondered nothingness.

I read the book *Autobiography of a Yogi* by Paramahansa Yogananda from cover to cover. Although I had started to read this meaningful book about a yogi's life and travels countless times at home, I had never finished it. But now I had the time and space to read and reflect. I began to acknowledge and appreciate each quiet moment, realizing that I never could have dreamed how fulfilling they would be. Being here on my own had allowed me to totally dive into a chant, a teaching, a reading, a quiet moment, even a cup of chai—fully, wholly—for days on end. It was almost surreal.

Prior to this, my days at home had been peppered with texts, phone calls, and messages from my daughters, family, and friends. Now I lived in uninterrupted space and gave myself the time and attention that often went to my children and others. I indulged my inner voice and followed it to deeper places of tranquility within. I felt the scales of balance in my life move toward my own inner fulfillment.

～

While I immersed myself in the ashram setting, some of my fellow classmates took short jaunts to nearby villages to shop and explore. I had no desire to join them. Maybe it was my total comfort at the ashram—or maybe, deep down, I didn't want to risk partaking in anything that might jeopardize the sense of security and comfort that I felt being in India on my own, without my family beside me. My boat didn't need to be rocked.

One of my friends left the ashram grounds on a semi-regular basis in order to see the sites. She didn't return with silky scarves or handmade statues, or sweet Indian treats like mango *kulfi* or coconut *ladoos*. She returned with chocolate, probably imported— the perfect item to share with a new friend from New York. People were allowed to bring outside food into the ashram, so it wasn't like she needed to sneak it in as contraband. But because I had no other way of getting it, it was just as exciting. Sometimes I would pay her for the chocolate. Other times, she would see me salivating at the thought of it, and she would toss a piece to me like she was feeding bread to a needy duck in a pond.

My spiritual and chocolate cravings were being satisfied at the ashram, and with each day, I was becoming more grateful for my time there and for the generosity of my fellow classmates. Their generosity wasn't limited to the sharing of chocolate. My friends also shared the deepest parts of themselves during each class and conversation, as did the instructors. I relished each day.

One afternoon, as I was walking to the dining hall, Annie stopped me.

"Isn't it great to be here?" Her eyes were beaming.

"It sure is," I replied. "But time is starting to zip by. It's like with our kids. One day, they're babies. The next day, they're in school."

"Or in college."

"Annie, don't even say that."

"I know, but it's true," she said. "We need to stop and cherish this moment right now because—just like with our kids—it will be gone before we know it."

"You're completely right. Let's remind each other to do just that whenever we think of it. We should just stop each other and say, 'Okay, cherish this moment.'"

From then on, as we crossed paths with one another during the remainder of our stay, Annie and I would often pull each other aside and whisper, "Cherish the moment." It brought all of our thoughts to that instant with appreciation and gratitude. Having seen our children grow overnight, both of us knew that everything good and bad passes by—and it's usually the good stuff that flies by.

Back at home, everything was running smoothly. "Things are just fine," Jim wrote in an email. He just left out the part about the record-breaking snowfall that hit New York while I basked in sunny weather and the company of new friends. He allowed me to partake in this experience without worry, knowing that I would surely come home if I thought he needed me—even if that meant persuading my chocolate-sharing, duck-feeding friend to help me. But clearly, there wasn't a need for that. Jim was managing our family and a very busy snowplowing business just fine.

I began to realize that my children could have their needs met by others and continue on without my physical presence to everyone's satisfaction. It didn't diminish any love or connection between us—maybe it even made it stronger. We were supportive of one another and resilient as mothers, as fathers, as children, as husband and wife. Although I didn't take this journey with the intention of realizing my family's strengths or their adaptability, that is exactly what floated to the surface.

FINDING BALANCE

BECAUSE I WAS in the heartland of yoga and able to contemplate God, life, death, and beyond with every ounce of my being and without any distraction, I experienced some of the most profound moments of my life. Up until this time, the births of my two children had been the most life-changing and awe-inspiring events that I had faced; while in India, I had experiences that rivaled those.

"Jesus, I felt like my leg was about to fall off in that last yoga class," I said, as I sat down at a small table at the ashram's intimate outdoor café.

"I didn't attempt any of those last few asanas," Kathy replied. "I was comfortable just standing there—with both feet on the ground."

"Let's just say if I had held the last one a second longer, not only would both my feet have been on the ground but the rest of my body as well," I laughed.

A few moments later, our conversation shifted from the movement of our physical bodies to the more subtle aspects of our being. I heard the beginning notes of the evening chant drifting in the still air from the temple, but I couldn't pull myself away from the deep conversation. I was too interested in the discussion and too relaxed in my seat to go anywhere.

When the yoga classes ended the following day, I felt like moving in a different direction. I avoided the lure of the cozy café and its captivating conversation and walked directly to the temple for the evening chant. I removed my shoes and placed them on the handmade wooden shelves. Then I stepped inside and sat down on the hard earth, drawing in the smoky incense that enveloped me. I surveyed the area and noticed that only a handful of my fellow classmates were present, along with only a few ashram residents, and about half the number of young Sanskrit students who attended school there. Since the crowd was minimal, I was grateful that I had come to lend my voice and presence to the chant.

I closed my eyes and heard someone begin to play the harmonium. Moments later, my voice joined with others, singing the mantra. As the tempo of the chant increased and the words came more rapidly, I heard the thunder of deep drumming begin to move along with the waves of music. I opened my eyes for a moment and noticed that Guruji had joined us, his nimble hands resonating on the taut skin of *tablas*, Indian drums that resemble large copper bowls with tops bound by twine. The young Sanskrit students who had come for the chant had moved into a circle alongside him in the middle of the temple. They were shaking maracas and clanging miniature cymbals to the beat.

I closed my eyes again and sang freely, as if I was singing my favorite song with no one around. I sang from the deepest parts of me, from my soul...and something incredible happened. I felt as if I became completely free of my entire physical body. I felt huge, like a part of everything, but that everything wasn't space. It was a feeling of love, of fullness, of wholeness. I still had some sense of myself but not a sense of me as the physical body. It was a sense of me as part of all this, the totality of everything. I hadn't disengaged so that I did not exist, but my sense of self stemmed from a knowing within the larger body of wholeness. I wasn't limited to the physical sense of me. I was an intricate part of everything, and everything wasn't shapes and forms. Everything was this sense of aliveness, of completeness. A concentrated energy existed within all this, emanating from the space where the intense drumming and chanting were coming from, in the middle of the temple where Guruji and the students sat. A kind of flowing took place between that center and where my sense of knowing existed.

The chant could have lasted a moment, an hour, a day. I felt no sense of time. When the chant slowed and finally ended, I gradually opened my eyes, completely moved forever. I had experienced a connection to something greater, outside of my limited body. I knew that we are all connected to, comprised of, this greatness. I knew it not only in my heart or head but deep down in my very essence. We are love and energy and completely whole. We are the wave that becomes the ocean and the ocean that becomes the wave.

I walked out of the temple in silence, wanting to cherish the experience without words or conversation. I wasn't ready to draw my attention to anything else, not even to the terms I would need to describe it to friends because I realized any description would pale in comparison to the true magnitude of the connection I felt beyond my individual existence. I wanted to hold on to the feeling and knowing deep inside me, embodying it for as long as I could.

About a week later, the ashram prepared to celebrate India's

Republic Day. It's celebrated in similar fashion to the Fourth of July in every small town in America but without the hotdogs and hamburgers. Guruji had been invited by a nearby elementary school to be an honored guest and to raise the Indian flag to begin the school's celebration. He asked a handful of young Sanskrit students and adult students from the yoga retreat to accompany him to the school, and surprisingly, I was asked to go.

Although I had kept myself within the confines of the ashram property based on my own volition, I filled with excitement at the prospect of exploring the nearby area. I felt as if the safeguard of the ashram would extend wherever Guruji went. I ran back to my room and only had time to grab my shawl before we headed out.

Once our group was on its way, we bounced along bumpy dirt roads lined by wide expanses of flat, dry earth and concrete buildings. Dust gathered on the outside walls of these structures, muting the vibrancy of their painted exteriors. The van slowed down as it entered a remote village. Minutes later, it followed a cement wall that led to the school's entranceway and stopped on the street in front of an open archway.

Our party filed out and walked directly onto a courtyard filled with about one hundred children who looked between the ages of five to twelve. The students were standing in lines that seemingly split according to age. They were dressed beautifully; the girls wore colorful skirts, and the boys dressed more uniformly in dark pants. Most of the girls had white jasmine buds interlaced in their hair, and they reminded me of my daughters back home.

The Sanskrit students who had come from the ashram returned to the van to unload boxes of food that had been brought as a donation while the younger children in the courtyard watched and giggled. A gentleman from the school, dressed semi-casually in loose white pants and a button-down shirt, came over and welcomed us in a foreign language. Then he led us to a row of metal chairs that faced the young pupils. I sat down slowly and began to observe my surroundings more fully.

The courtyard before me was comprised of dry dirt and scattered patches of grass. Two of its' sides were fenced in by the white concrete wall that we had followed driving up to the entrance, and a short, one-story building lined the remaining sides. As I gazed around the space, a small group of students, standing in the center, drew my attention with their boisterous laughter. I watched them as they tried to stifle themselves and become more inconspicuous, and I found that I couldn't look away. They kept my attention until Guruji walked to the flag pole and raised the Indian flag. After the cheers subsided, another group of children walked to one end of the yard and began to dance. Their movements were quick and in sync, and my eyes were mesmerized by their joy and enthusiasm. As other groups of young entertainers followed, I couldn't help but become enamored with each and every one of them.

It cannot be measured in degrees, but it used to seem that the love I had for Kailee and Paige was special—something that only a mother could have for her own children. And it also seemed as if I had a deeper level of caring for all of those children who I knew personally. But after bathing in a pool of love at the ashram— speaking, learning, and living in an environment of total peace and serenity, talking of God and our connection to each other, to all— I looked at the children in front of me with the same eyes and same feeling that I looked at my own daughters with. I gazed at them with undeniable love. I knew then that there was no difference between these children and my own. The love ran just as deep. The only differentiation lay in the recipient of my sentiment, not in the feeling itself. With this realization, I was overcome with emotion; all I could do was cry with a completely open heart.

This short trip to a rural school—where I knew no child, could not understand any words spoken—went beyond language.

It ripped my heart open and allowed every one of those children to jump inside.

AS MY TIME at the ashram was winding down, a part of me grew excited at the thought of wrapping my arms around my family again, and a part of me wished I could stay longer. I walked out of my room and leaned over the metal railing that lined the open hallway of my accommodation. The scenery in front of me would be different within days. *Yes, Annie, the good stuff really does fly by*, I mused.

A friend waved to me from the ground below and headed up the concrete steps to chat. As soon as he climbed the last step, I saw the broad smile of the tall Australian man whose company I had come to appreciate over the last month. Alex was a friendly guy in his early forties whose tan, rough skin and receding hairline made him look older than he really was. Throughout our time together, his Aussie accent and lingo had provided me with tons of material for some good-natured ribbing.

"G'day, mate," I said, in an Australian accent I hadn't quite perfected.

"G'day," Alex replied, grinning. "I can't believe we'll be going home in a few days."

"I know. In some ways, I feel like I just got here, and in other ways, I feel like I've always been here."

"I know what you mean," Alex agreed. "A few of us decided to soak in the last couple of days in India with a trip to the village where Bhagavan lived. We're leaving the ashram a day early to explore it. We'll sleep over and head to the airport from there. Care to join us?"

The destination was the temple and former residence of the Indian saint whose image was embodied in the golden statues that sat in Guruji's ashrams in India and New York. In the family tree of gurus, he had a grandfatherly connection to Guruji, without any biological relation. He was the guru of Guruji's guru and was often referred to as *Bhagavan*, meaning *Lord* or *God*, out of reverence, a practice often followed in regard to saintly beings in India. Although I never met Bhagavan while he was alive, I had spent countless hours in front of his image at both ashrams, and his life and teachings had been the focus of countless contemplations.

I considered the opportunity. Maybe this trip would allow me to feel even closer to him, like visiting a friend in his own home, in his own surroundings—feeling his presence, sensing his way of life, grasping his roots.

"Yes," I replied. "That sounds awesome."

Days later, I said goodbye to my classmates, friends, and soul mates. Each hug that I gave and each one that I received seemed to have its own conversation. Each one told its own story. Some lasted only a few moments while others went on for minutes; our embraces embodying our shared time together. The only common denominators in all of them were love and gratitude. On some deeper level, there was also an appreciative recognition of some shared purpose for coming together. Although our trips were sparked by different reasons, there was something common among us—a willingness to spend time with strangers at an ashram, an openness to diverse thoughts and feelings in our shared search for answers, a feeling of community that included all of humanity.

After I said my final farewell, I stepped into the timeworn van and left the ashram with my traveling companions. Our journey lasted only a few hours, but it allowed me to glimpse a view of India different from the one I knew at the ashram. As we traveled down potholed dirt roads, I saw families sitting under tarps and seemingly living in impermanent structures. Metal bowls, cloth items, and pieces of cardboard were all that I could discern under these tiny shelters. Cows and elephants freely roamed the roads and barren fields while isolated trees endured the dry, arid land. It was the complete opposite of the lush green setting that I had just departed from.

I began to appreciate my time at the ashram and my life at home on a greater scale, but I also began to feel ashamed. I had taken so much for granted: tasty meals, clean clothes, even my comfy bed. I offered a silent prayer of gratitude for all that I had and one of apology for a lifetime of ungraciousness.

Hours later, our van turned between two stone pillars capping a wrought iron gate and stopped in front of a white, two-story building. The beveled roof and open hallways on the second floor reminded me of the ashram.

"We're here," Alex said. "This is where we'll stay tonight. It's the closest thing to a motel around. We'll check in, drop our luggage, and then head to Bhagavan's temple."

"Sounds like a plan," I replied.

We took our luggage from the back of the van and walked through an open doorway into a foyer that felt tropical with tall, potted plants lining cream-colored walls. A friend registered us at the front desk, and then a beautiful Indian woman dressed in a long, pink tunic and loose pants led us to our rooms.

After she led Alex and a handful of others to their rooms, she walked me to mine. As she opened the door, my eyes scanned a simple, sparsely decorated room. Dark cobwebs hung in the corners of the concrete walls giving me the impression that they had been there for years. The walls had once been painted white, but time or inattention had allowed large patches of their natural clay color to break through. The bed—a thin mattress atop a metal frame covered by a multi-colored blanket—rested against a wall, adjacent to a doorless archway leading to the bathroom. The desk clerk smiled and handed the key to me.

"Thank you," I offered. "Namaste."

After the woman left, I bent down and firmly tugged at the zippers of my luggage, ensuring the tightest seal and maximum block against anything that might come slithering by. Then I stepped outside and met up with my friends.

"How is your room?" Alex asked, raising his eyebrows.

"It will be fine for the night, but I think Bhagavan himself may have been the last person who stayed there. It looks like it hasn't seen the light of day in years."

"Mine too," Alex chuckled. "It's like we've stepped back in time."

"True, but on some level, simpler times have an appeal all their own."

"They sure do."

As we walked toward Bhagavan's temple, the unpaved streets became lined with shanty lean-tos that were overflowing with religious items and souvenirs for sale. Silver necklaces fancied with charms of gods and goddesses lay on tables between rich, earth-colored mala beads. Gold and silver statues of other divine beings encircled the tables with framed pictures of saints resting below. A merchant beckoned us to stop and take a closer look at his religious wares while an old woman, whose legs seemed to have disappeared under the ripples of a dirt-stained skirt, sat on the road, begging for alms. Dust whirled around us almost constantly.

The street was busier than I expected, and I was surprised by the myriad people walking by me. Some wore traditional Indian clothing—women in colorful saris and flowing scarves, men in long shirts and loincloths; while others donned more familiar Western styles—spacious tunics and pants. The potpourri of outfits reflected the melting pot of people and cultures around me, and I began to realize the extent of this great yogi's draw, flowing far beyond the dirt roads and rural ways of this tiny Indian village.

As we drew closer to the temple, the earth below my feet was laid with smooth stone blocks, and my heart began to beat faster with anticipation. A moment later, my eyes met the tall, white pillars standing guard before the entrance. Statues of Hindu gods and goddesses adorned the spaces above the columns, as if protecting the majesty that lay inside, and I felt as if I was at the feet of royalty.

As I entered the temple, I smelled burning incense and recognized the huge, golden statue sitting at the far end. The statue of Bhagavan was the same image that sat in Guruji's ashrams. It was sheltered under the umbrella of an ornate, sterling, dome-like structure and sat on top of a massive stand that looked as if it was made of stone and silver. Unlike the altars within Guruji's ashrams, a short wall separated the sacred space where the figure sat from the area where one could sit and chant or meditate.

I felt my connection to Bhagavan immediately. I felt a connection deeper than just a subtle recognition of a golden statue. I felt a connection to a path whose history was embodied in the dirt roads I had just walked, in the temple I now stood, and in the people who surrounded me.

I looked back at the endless stream of people walking through the doors of the temple. It almost seemed too busy for me to become quiet and steady, even if I closed my eyes, but I knew I had to try. I wanted to feel still and one with this saint, this lineage of gurus, and everything around me. I sat down on the hard rug, crossed my legs, and closed my eyes. I heard people in conversation all around me. I heard the rumblings of constant movement. I didn't feel the profoundly deeper communion that I hoped for.

Was it the place, the physical space I was in? Or was it where I was—mentally, emotionally—almost headed home and outside of the shelter of the ashram? I waited a few minutes. Then I leaned toward Alex.

"I'm heading out," I whispered. "I'll catch up with you later." With his eyes still closed, he nodded his head in understanding.

I followed the crowd and walked back through the embellished opening and onto the flat stone blocks that surrounded the entrance. Within moments, my feet touched the dry earth of the unpaved road again. As I strolled, I looked for the vanilla-colored, two-story house that was said to have been Bhagavan's residence at one time. Since his death, his home was open to the public. I stopped in front of the only building in the area fitting the description and glanced over a wooden sign posted in front. A moment later, I found the word "Bhagavan" amidst other foreign words and assumed that this was the place where he had spent years meditating, being one with the One.

The house looked as if it was made of cement—solid, unmovable—and I wondered whether its sturdiness stemmed from the hard material it was made of or from the years of sacred practice it imbibed. I walked through a gated entranceway into an open hallway and immediately felt an inner ease, like the comfort I felt inside the ashram at the retreat. I felt at home in my heart and closer to Bhagavan than when I sat in his temple.

A man dressed in milky-white-colored clothing walked toward me. He was small in stature and wore a snug-fitting, sailor-like hat. From a distance, he looked like India's version of *Popeye*, prior to any spinach-eating escapade.

"Namaste. Welcome," he said, with his palms together.

"Namaste," I replied, bowing my head slightly.

He motioned for me to follow him as he led me into a completely empty room off of the exposed hallway. I imagined the room as it may have looked in Bhagavan's time—filled with people dressed in jewel-toned clothing. In my mind, they were singing and dancing as they encircled the room in an ecstatic chant. I could almost see the thick fog of incense that may have floated then, muting their brilliant attire but not their joyous sounds or movements. I let the full picture take shape, silently chanting *Hare Ram, Hare Krishna* to myself.

A few moments later, my guide motioned for us to head back to the hallway and into another room just a few steps away. I peered into a tiny room about a quarter of the size of the previous one. The walls were white and without any decoration. A single piece of furniture—a flat wooden bench or bed without any cushion—rested against one of the walls.

"This is where he meditated," my guide said in broken English.

I closed my eyes for a moment and imagined Bhagavan sitting in front of me, sharing the sacred space. I waited a minute, hoping to be led to another room, but quickly realized that was it—only two rooms on tour. Instantly, I felt a child-like desire to dash away to explore the rest of the residence on my own. I swallowed the impulse, and instead, reached into my pocket and gave some coins to my guide. He accepted the money graciously, drew his hands together, and bowed his head.

"Namaste," he said again.

"Namaste," I replied.

Although both rooms lacked any ornamentation, they seemed full of life in my mind and heart. I looked back down the airy hallway we had just come from and glimpsed an oversized, wooden chair that my guide and I had walked by as we went from one room to the other. I recognized the wide arms of the chair from a picture I had seen. In the picture, Bhagavan had been seated on the chair with one arm in the air seemingly blessing those around him. I walked over and sat in front of it, leaning my back against a short block wall. I closed my eyes and felt quiet. My mind did not go anywhere. It remained with my breath in the moment.

When I was ready to leave, I opened my eyes and walked back to the dirt street. I had no idea how long I had been sitting. No one had bothered me. I hadn't heard any outside conversation or chatter. I had been able to grasp the fullness of the quiet moments that I sat in.

What was it about his home that allowed me to grow still and feel more connected to him? Was it the humbler setting without the golden statue and flock of people? Was it the tranquil space that allowed me to grow quieter? Or, for a few moments, had I just allowed myself to let go of any expectation, any thought, and any anticipation of my upcoming trek home? Whatever the reason, I filled with gratitude for being able to sit and walk in the footsteps of someone so wise. As I walked down the street, I held on to the calm and quiet within and embraced my connection to a rich line of gurus and seekers.

I walked back between the stone pillars at the entrance of my motel and followed a path lined by tall, green grass. Natural hot springs nearby nourished the vegetation. I continued walking beyond my accommodation down a mild embankment.

As I looked over my shoulder, I saw a huge mountain in the distance and became mesmerized by it. It was wide and squatty and dotted with tropical trees. It reminded me of an asana that I had practiced in the yoga classes at the ashram—*tadasana*, the mountain pose. The mountain exuded strength and stability and seemed the epitome of complete balance. As I gazed at it, *tadasana* became more than a mere physical posture, a reference to standing tall on two feet. It was a feeling, a sense of strength of being, and I knew that I needed to take that awareness back home with me.

I walked away from the mountain elated. I felt as if I was becoming the walking embodiment of *tadasana* now. I was grounded in my beliefs and felt a sense of balance within me. The mountain began to represent the culmination of a journey that went beyond mere miles traveled. It represented the goal of the journey within.

FINDING BALANCE

V

WEAVING A BEAUTIFUL TAPESTRY

FINDING BALANCE

36

AFTER I SLID my Liz Claiborne carry-on below the seat in front of me, I relaxed back and closed my eyes. Soon I would be holding my children, drawing in the familiar fragrance of shampoo lingering in their hair, and feeling my husband's strong arms wrap around me. Five weeks apart had flown by for me, and I hoped that my family felt the same or at least in the relative ballpark.

Before I embarked on this trip, I assumed that the biggest adjustment would occur during the first few days in India as I grew accustomed to living each day without my family beside me. But as I recalled how I had eased into relative comfort at the ashram, embracing the schedule and a lifestyle focused wholly on spirit, I realized that I had not considered the shift returning home. I was going back to televisions, playful chatter, and the business of my family.

How I could realistically bridge the world centered on my inner self with the one centered on my family? I wondered. I wanted to hold on to this sense of balance and fullness back home, and I knew that it would take effort. Meditation and chanting would have to become regular parts of my daily life like my morning coffee, or more recently, cup of chai. I resolved to make them part of my routine. I started to feel hopeful that a more balanced way of living was in the cards for me now, especially since my plan for home felt like the natural progression of the path I was already on.

I gazed out the cabin window and smiled as I eyed the time—only fifteen more hours.

The flight home was smooth, and my walk through customs was uneventful. As I walked down the airport corridor, I spotted my family at the end, just beyond security. Kailee and Paige were wearing puffy winter coats, and Jim was sporting the white Calvin Klein sweater that I had given him for Christmas. The girls were standing behind a stroller that was too small for them but perfect for the doll and bouquet of flowers it now held.

I started to run, but I couldn't get to them fast enough for my melting heart. When I reached them, I dropped my bags and felt my daughters cinch around my waist. Jim brought his arms around all of us and kissed me directly on the mouth. It felt like I had never left.

As I released my embrace, Jim smiled as he looked into my eyes. Deep-down, I knew that my eyes probably looked the same and, except for the beautiful henna on my hands, so did my outside body, but the inner being behind all that had changed. I was back in New York not only in one piece but at peace with a deeper appreciation and connection to all that is.

I took Paige's hand, and we began to push the stroller together. I drew my other arm around Kailee while Jim retrieved my luggage and walked alongside us. The girls began asking me about my plane ride and India, and I began asking them about snow days and school. Tears came to my eyes as we walked toward the car. I realized how naïve I had been over the years thinking that

I would be the one providing my children and family with opportunities for growth, because as I looked at them, I knew that was the gift they had given to me.

When we reached the car, I sensed that life would return to normal soon, but I was also certain that my everyday life would be different. I had tasted the heart of India and walked a path toward my own spiritual fulfillment. I knew, in my very essence, that we are the ocean that becomes the wave and the wave that becomes the ocean—and that knowing changes everything.

On the ride home, Kailee and Paige began showering me with stories about all of the activities they were involved in while I was away: sleigh riding, snowplowing with their dad, trips to friends' homes, and even Kailee's birthday celebration with Ellie and Mike.

"Mom, it even snowed on my birthday," Kailee bubbled. "It snowed so much that our school closed down for my birthday. Can you believe it? They closed school for my birthday!"

We laughed out loud, and I savored the sound of my children's laughter, cherishing it like I was hearing their voices for the first time.

"Wow, Kailee," I said, not able to stop smiling. "That's so cool. Do you think they'll do that for you too, Paige?"

"Probably not, Mom—unless you move my birthday to December." Paige rolled her eyes, giving us more reason to laugh out loud.

As I looked outside the frosty windows of the car, I noticed all of the huge piles of snow on the ground. Jim had to juggle a lot of balls while I was away: snow plowing, dinners, laundry, the girls, his business, whatever. He never shared any feelings of stress or overwhelm with me, if he ever even felt those, nor did he ever make me feel guilty about being away. He never gave me any shit for taking a journey thousands of miles away from him and our children, and I filled with gratitude. I grabbed his hand.

"Thank you," I whispered.

He gazed over at me and squeezed my hand. Things had been absolutely fine while I was away. Everyone had survived and maybe even flourished. Jim had managed without me, mother and wife, and we were just fine, too.

When we arrived home, I walked inside and found the entire first floor of our home decorated with hand-drawn pictures, flowers, and crepe paper. "Welcome Home" signs were hung on cabinets, doors, chairs, everywhere. And then my eyes spotted the dirty tissues lying in the same bowl that my daughters had placed them in before I left.

"Well guys, I think this is the best surprise of all," I laughed, holding up the bowl. "You kept my dead tissues."

"See, Mom. We told you," Paige said. "We didn't throw them away."

"We held on to them, Mom—just like we said we would," Kailee added.

I wanted to tell them that I had held on to each one of them in my heart the whole time I was away too—just like the tissues— but I didn't want to start crying. I knew that my family had felt our connection.

"You guys are the best," I said. "I love you both." I walked over and drew my girls close.

Jim walked over and put his arms around all of us, squeezing us tightly. "So glad you're home," he said, affectionately.

Exhaustion began to set in after a couple of hours since my body was still on India time. I ended up falling asleep on the couch while the girls snuggled in my arms. Hours later, I woke to the sounds of the television and the quiet chatter of little girls playing house. The noises around me no longer held sacred sounds from melodious chants or the laughter of young boys playing cricket. I smiled inside, appreciating where I had been and where I was now. *I'm home.*

The next morning, I felt a chill in the air and looked over my shoulder to see that Paige had bundled herself up in the covers, leaving only the edges of the blankets available to everyone else. Our family had decided to sleep together in our king-sized bed just as we did the night before I began this journey.

As I slowly untucked a blanket from under Paige, I heard her whisper, "Mom, can we stay home from school today?" Kailee lifted her head from the bottom of our bed and folded her hands pleadingly.

"Of course, we definitely need a day together."

"Yeah," they replied, snuggling deeper into the covers.

Jim smiled at me from across the bed. "Wish I could stay home, too, but I have a lot of work today."

"I completely understand. Go get ready and I'll make some breakfast."

After Jim left for work, the morning flew by as I unpacked, played house, did laundry, and pretended to eat eggs, bacon, cake, and spaghetti from the girls' little kitchen. When lunchtime came, I decided to make grilled cheese sandwiches, hoping to maintain the vegetarian diet I had followed at the ashram and ignore the salami and prosciutto that called to me each time I opened the refrigerator door.

While the buttery sandwiches toasted in the pan, I noticed that the television was on in the family room without anyone watching it. I interrupted the preparation of a three-tier plastic cake and asked Kailee to shut it off. Then I wondered if I would have noticed that before.

When the sandwiches were done, we sat at the kitchen table and ate our lunch with our hands. Sure, we had always eaten grilled cheese sandwiches with our hands before, but this time I relished the feeling.

"Doesn't the bread feel so crispy in your hands?"

"I guess," Kailee said.

"Yeah, like it usually does, Mom," Paige added.

"Yeah, I guess so, too…like usual. It just feels really warm and crispy. My cheese is all melted, and it feels so gooey, too."

Paige and Kailee looked at each other. "The cheese is usually gooey, Mom," Kailee said.

"You're right. I guess I just haven't had grilled cheese in a while," I said, bringing the sandwich to my lips.

I had held on to that feeling of mindfulness—embracing the moment with all my senses. Sure, my daughters probably thought that I had lost my mind because they always seemed to live in the present moment. They knew that the bread felt crispy, and the cheese was gooey. They didn't realize that I was just getting back to that innocent, grateful recognition and appreciation of being and living each moment more fully. Slowly, I was noticing, something within me had changed. I could appreciate all the tiny nuances that even a sandwich could offer. I was satisfied. I was content. Wholly content…with a grilled cheese sandwich.

I began to carry that fresh perspective and awareness into my daily activities. Before I folded the clothes, I put them up to my face and felt the lingering heat from the dryer. When I played house with the girls, I allowed my mind to stay in the game and not head to plans for dinner. My whole being had slowed down. I wasn't moving through the day's activities without a fullness of being. I embraced the present moment; I felt like I had found the recipe for a sweeter, richer day.

I also started taking advantage of the quiet moments. Each morning, I woke up before Kailee and Paige to sit by myself, thoughtfully repeat the mantra, and meditate. I treasured those few moments alone. No matter how much I gave to my children, my husband, my family, I knew how important it was to take that time for me. I needed to balance my family's needs with my own, and I felt like I had a greater handle on the rhythms of my internal scale.

As time went on and months went by, my daily tasks became more routine. I did not hold the clothes from the dryer to my face before I folded them. I didn't automatically notice the crispiness of the bread on my grilled cheese sandwich or the gooeyness of the cheese. I ate the salami and the prosciutto. Although it wasn't always as easy to notice on the outside anymore, I still held on to the feeling of oneness that I experienced in the chant and the feeling of love that I felt for strangers at the Indian school. I held on to a deeper appreciation and feeling of gratitude for everyone and everything around me. On some level, I held on to my connection to something greater. It was more than a thought, more than a feeling; that insight was a part of me.

Soon after my return home, Paige noticed a rose-colored bracelet made of yarn encircling one of my wrists. It stood out among the other silver ones that dangled.

"Mommy, where did you get that red bracelet?" Paige asked, pointing to my wrist.

"I received it at a ceremony that I took part in at the ashram in India. All of the people there received one. I think it's just like a reminder of the love and blessings that we received." I struggled to recall a deeper meaning for the bracelet but realized I had never asked anyone before. Now I wished I had.

"Can I make a friendship bracelet for you to wear on your wrist too, Mom? Kailee taught me how to make them." Paige's eyes widened with excitement.

"Of course you can. I would love that."

A short time later, Paige walked into the kitchen with a blue, purple, and black, braided friendship bracelet in hand.

"Here you go," she said, proudly.

"I love it, Paige. It's awesome. Thank you. Do you think I should wear it on the same wrist that has the red bracelet on it or the other one?"

"The same one," she replied, without hesitation.

"Okay, then that's where I'll wear it." I tied the bracelet on immediately.

Months have passed and both bracelets look like threads from an old sweater, but something interesting has started happening to them. One of the threads from Paige's band has begun to wrap itself around the one from the ashram as if it was weaving itself into the other; the bracelets seemingly supporting each other.

As I look at these bracelets now, I realize that this is how all facets of life should come together. Career, marriage, motherhood, spirituality—every thread in life's beautiful tapestry—must weave in and out, creating new patterns and blends that invite change and inspire personal growth. Frosty mugs and light conversation had to make room for chai and loftier discussions as I realized my own changing needs. In the end, I needed to recognize the things that offered me a more lasting feeling of contentment and entwine them more fully into my life. It was then that I rested on the solid foundation of the mountain and felt balanced, availing myself of the treasures within.

FINDING BALANCE

GRATITUDE

I THANK THE UNIVERSE each time my eyes dance in the beautiful sky that a sunset leaves behind. I thank the universe each time my children are late coming home but arrive safely. I thank the universe each time I see the smiling faces around me and know that I am surrounded by kind, loving people. I thank the universe for grilled cheese sandwiches, crispy bread, and gooey cheese. I am grateful for everything.

I am moved to mention some of the people in my life who have guided me and showered me with the generosity of their hearts, their wisdom, and their understanding.

My Guru and his lineage taught me something that goes beyond words and feelings. They shared the path to my own wholeness. There are no words that can offer enough thanks, no actions that can satisfy my need to offer them my deepest gratitude. I can only *pranaam* with every part of me.

My parents, Sandy and Tom Swierski, gave the gift of life to me and offer their eternal guidance. Growing up in their arms along-side my brother Scott taught me the meaning of family.

My husband, Jim, carries me with his love and support every day. His encouragement gave me the strength and opportunity to pursue my dreams, and his devotion to our family shows our daughters the kind of person one should try to be. He rocks my world on every level.

My children, Kailee Faithe and Paige Alyssa, teach me through their unconditional love and weave a fuller sense of joy into each day. They are the jewels of my life.

My friend, Devayani (Kimberly Cable), devotes her life to the path of yoga, to the path of devotion. We are connected on the deepest levels, and her friendship and guidance always come wrapped in exuberance. She is my sister in my heart.

My friend, Girija (Kathy Quick), opened the door to meditation and yoga for me. She took me by the hand and introduced me to people, places, and paths that changed my life forever. She is both a guide in life and one of my dearest friends.

My friend, Donna Goldberger, laughs with me, cries with me, and provides me with unwavering support and encouragement like no other. She continues to be brave enough to trek into the unknown with me.

My friend, Mo-z (Maureen Wassermann), has spent untold hours with me on park benches and picnic blankets. We share a friendship that stems from our core and always feels natural and effortless. She is my soul sister.

My extended family and friends show me the sweet meaning of kinship and support no matter how many miles separate us. We will be connected for lifetimes.

My editor, Laura Duggan, posed profound questions that allowed me to dig deeper. Her insight and thoughtfulness brought clarity to many elements of my journey.

I honor each one of these loving individuals and thank them from the deepest parts of me.

I am grateful to each person whom I've met in every place that I've journeyed.

May all of us weave a beautiful tapestry with life's changing threads as we continue to find balance within.

Peace.

Made in the USA
Middletown, DE
09 December 2020